Selling Your Handcrafts

WILLIAM E. GARRISON

•••••●●●●●●●•••••

SELLING YOUR HANDCRAFTS

CHILTON BOOK COMPANY
Radnor, Pennsylvania

Designed by Adrianne Onderdonk Dudden

Manufactured in the United States of America

Library of Congress Cataloging in Publication Data

Garrison, William E.
  Selling your handcrafts.

  1. Salesmen and salesmenship—handicraft.
I. Title.
HF5439.H27G37   1974   658.89'7455   74-16304
ISBN 0-8019-6042-8
ISBN 0-8019-6043-6 (pbk.)

Contents

Introduction

So you have a new hobby! You are starting creative work in any one of many handcrafts: bottle cutting, candles, stained glass, ceramics, jewelry, or egg craft. You are going to "do your own thing" while enjoying the release of tension, the self-satisfaction of creativity, the expression of the "real you."

That's great. By all means get into it as quickly as possible, along with the several million other Americans who have a similar urge. Get your equipment, supplies, and instruction, and start.

It won't be long until you are producing your own work. And you will be proud that it is indeed your own work. You will show your first results to anyone who expresses interest and explain that you did this all by yourself.

As your skill increases, you will improve not only in quality of work but also in output. Some of these expressions of your creativity will be given away to friends and to relatives for birthdays, anniversaries, and for Christmas gifts. Those who receive the gifts will properly compliment you on the perfection of detail and the skill with which you executed the design.

You will glow with these compliments, as indeed you should. Your newly acquired skills will become even more important to you than they were in the beginning. You will go back for more classes and spend more time in your shop, because you have been motivated to do an even better job in the future.

But one day you will pause and wonder, "What can I use as a gift next time? I have already given two or three of the kind of thing I'm doing now. Next time it's going to have to be something quite different."

Stop right now and face up to it. There is a limit to the number of things you can give away. What are you going to do with the results of your handcraft when you have given away all that you can gracefully give? Are you going to build a barn in which to store them? Are they simply going to pile up wherever there is a bit of room? Or is there a better way?

Now you are facing up to the real problem: what are you going to *do* with your handcrafts? It's great to have a burning desire to produce fine handwork; everything about that goal is good. But in the end, what are you going to *do* with your handcrafts?

Eventually it comes to this: you must sell that part of your handcrafts which is surplus to your needs. There just isn't anything else to do. It doesn't make sense to throw these things away. How can you store them, or make further use of these items as gifts? So it comes to the point where you must start selling or quit producing!

Take a good look at this statement. Walk

around it and look at it from every side: start selling or quit producing!

If you have any other answer, it will be most surprising. For there comes a time when your enthusiasm over your new hobby will die a sudden death unless you begin disposing of what you are producing. And when you run out of all other possibilities, it is time to face up to the need of making room for new creations by getting rid of some of the previous ones. If you can't give them away gracefully you can only: (1) store them; (2) junk them; (3) sell them.

Certainly the idea of selling your work is more acceptable than either of the other possibilities.

At this point, there is almost inevitably an objection. "But my work isn't *good enough* to sell."

This objection is not only to be expected, it's a very healthy reaction. If you have the kind of ego that leads you to believe that everything you do is not only likely to sell but to sell at high prices, you just don't belong among the rest of us mortals. A bit of honest humility is right and proper when you are just getting into a new hobby. When you look at your efforts and compare them with that of master craftsmen in the same field, you know you have done little more than make a blundering beginning. Thus it is honest to object that perhaps the work is not saleable.

The fact is that the beginning craftsman can sell his work, often starting with the very first finished pieces. However, since what I am suggesting is, basically, a venture into the world of commerce, it is essential that such a step be taken only with a thorough understanding of what is involved. Certainly, a measure of self-confidence will come from such an understanding.

The objective of this book is twofold. First, we are going to look in great detail into some of the ways to overcome your natural reluctance to put your work up for sale. I can prove to you that it is entirely proper and has been done by many before you. The beginning craftsman *can* sell his work. Second, this book attempts to define the necessary methods by which you can sell your work successfully. By this I mean that if you follow correct pricing methods and develop a positive attitude, you can become self-supporting through the sale of your crafts.

In the following case history I actually knew the person involved; we'll call him Mike. He had never been happy in a nine-to-five job. In fact, what he actually wanted to do was to make jewelry. If he had not believed in himself and persisted, we might never have heard the following success story. Straightaway, you have two essential factors: he wanted to learn a craft, and he believed in himself—his attitude was positive.

Luckily for Mike, he came into contact with a group of jewelers who were producing handcrafted work. They agreed to give him a chance to see what he could produce. The first results were far from promising. It turned out that Mike had great difficulty handling delicate work. His hands just didn't function well in such situations. When he attempted to work with wax models, the chances were better than even that he would wreck them.

It might have been considered an impossible situation. Mike, however, was eager. He really wanted to learn jewelry craft. So, instead of highly detailed, delicate work, he was assigned to pieces that called for little attention to fine detail.

His instructions were, "Hammer and forge bracelets and chains from copper and brass. Make them look truly handcrafted. Use random patterns and textures." He was given little more than introductory instruction, there was no time to hold his hand. "Here are the tools. See what you can do . . . just turn loose your creativity without taking too much time planning what you intend to create."

It turned out that this type of work was exactly what Mike was most suited for. Some might well call his work crude. To others it could look primitive or powerful. Rough, yes. It certainly did not look like anything produced by a machine. Mike hammered and forged his bracelets and all the time wondered, "Is my work good enough to sell?"

By the time Mike had created quite a few pieces, a local art festival loomed on the horizon. His work was offered for sale at a price that allowed for the time he had put into it. To Mike's surprise, his work sold. In fact, it sold so well that very little was left over at the end of the festival. Mike was overjoyed—he had copies made of that first check and passed them out among his friends.

The circumstances of this event are not at all unusual. A person who has just begun in a craft *can* sell his work. Eventually, he must make that choice: either start selling or quit producing. In my opinion, and this is based on years of experience in the field of handcrafted jewelry, it is remarkably easy to start selling—once you understand the various steps involved.

One vital point must be kept in mind: the question of whether or not any handproduced item is "worth selling" is not one that can be answered by the craftsman himself. Neither his teacher, nor an art critic, nor textbook theories can foretell accurately whether an item will sell. The question is answered by the buying public.

Obviously, if under reasonable conditions your work does not sell, then it may not have been good enough. But let us assume that circumstances were favorable. If the price was fair and it does sell, then you have to admit that your judgment was wrong. Your handcrafted work *was* good enough to sell. Keep in mind that the work must be exposed to a considerable number of potential buyers. It will not take long to get some evidence concerning "buyer response."

1

The Highest Hurdles: Ego and Attitude

The sale of craft materials, kits, tools, and equipment now amounts to a billion dollars annually in the United States. A major hardware chain in the Pacific Northwest has just added an arts and crafts section to each of their many retail stores. The interest in handcrafts has never been higher. Despite this great public interest, however, it often is not easy for the craftsperson to get started selling his work. Probably, the majority of handcrafted items produced in the United States will never be offered for sale. Many individuals switch from one hobby to another after a very short time. Since there are so many, there is no danger of running out of new hobbies. Much of this jumping from one hobby to another is due to the fact that many individuals have never learned how to sell their work. At that certain point when they must either start selling or stop producing, they stop producing and change to a new hobby.

This country annually imports hundreds of millions of dollars worth of handcrafted products from all over the world. Even in the most underdeveloped nations, the native handcrafters have efficient marketing systems readily available, systems that will buy local handcrafted work and sell it internationally.

In the United States, marketing opportunities are frequently limited to what the craftsperson can do on his own. Usually it is difficult to get help on how to price work, obtain licenses, and prepare tax returns. Local and regional associations and leagues do exist (see Chapter 11). Unfortunately, such organizations are often interested in the known artist and may be openly hostile to the beginner.

The craftsperson who sells his work moves from the ranks of amateur to semiprofessional. The question of whether or not the craftsperson is a professional does not hinge upon education, acceptance by associations or leagues, recognition by professional critics, or awards won. If the sale of his work provides his major source of income, then he is in business as a professional craftsman.

Later in the book, pricing and marketing of your own handcrafts are discussed in depth. Before we delve into those concrete facts, however, we must talk about the question of philosophy. Several major hurdles confront the beginning craftsman and, to make the task even more difficult, they are interwoven:

1. Ego;
2. Attitude—yours and that of the buying public;
3. An understanding of what handcrafts are.

The beginner must realize that it is perfectly normal for the novice to be reluctant to expose his work—and himself—to the buying public. Once he has overcome this natural fear of loss of face, he must develop a positive attitude.

The dictionary usually defines handcraft as an art, craft, or trade in which the skilled use of one's hands is required. Handcrafts should not look machine-made. Their irregularities of workmanship is what sets them apart from the items coming off the factory production line at a mile a minute. Apart from many other considerations, there is also the further differentiation between the fine arts and the crafts. It is not absolutely necessary for someone to have studied at art college for them to be able to produce objects of beauty in, say, wood, ceramics, or various metals. A certain amount of prestige is accorded artists in the fine arts—perhaps because of their many years of study at recognized educational institutions.

However, those in the fine arts can produce work that puzzles, outrages, stimulates, or depresses the viewer. While the merit of such work has been debated through the centuries, the artist's integrity is rarely challenged. However, all too frequently, the work of those in handcrafts is disparaged. All too often, the public forgets to approach each craft item with a fresh eye and accept it for what it is. Perhaps it is an attractive item, perhaps it is decorative or functional. Is it something a little different, an abstract shape in metal that is pleasing and stimulating?

Whether it is a handmade candle or a unique ceramic bowl, the handcrafted item deserves respect. Little thought is given by the public to the obvious merits of handcrafted items. Fortunately, the very fact that such items do sell nowadays, and sell well, is proof that people do appreciate them.

There are various reasons why many handcrafters never offer any of their work for sale. Perhaps their explanation sounds very logical. "It would take all of the fun out of it for me." Or, "If I sold anything I made, it would become work instead of a hobby." Once in a while you will hear, "I just cannot bear to part with anything I have worked on so hard."

Such explanations may well be true—at least partially true. Certainly there are always exceptions to the rule. I know of a craftsman in the Northwest whose work is internationally recognized. Certainly he ranks among the top in his field. None of this artist's work is for sale, despite good offers. This artist prefers to live on a limited income and keep all of the masterpieces—and they are truly that. Of course, this action could be construed as somewhat selfish; work that is really great should in some way be made available to inspire others.

Then there is the not too unusual case of the craftsman who is in a high income bracket, who obviously does not need additional income. If this affluent craftsman gains satisfaction from working with his hands, perhaps he does prefer to donate rather than sell his work. However, if he drives a hard bargain in his daily business, if he is known to be hard to part from his dollars, does he really like the idea of giving anything away? Most of the time, the businessman-craftsman who will not think of selling his own work is bluffing. He may even have convinced himself of the validity of his explanation. The truth of the matter is that he does not want to face reality. Whether these fears are acknowledged or buried in the subconscious, we all want to avoid:

1. A situation where we are made to feel ridiculous or are openly laughed at in public or semipublic;

2. An event in which we are "put in our place" by someone who is recognized as an authority. This differs from (1) above in that the first situation does not involve anyone of recognized stature. The re-

sultant feeling is much the same in both cases, but it stems from different sources;

3. An occasion when we have to face up to the fact that we made a major error in judgment, not just missing the mark a little . . . missing the whole target area. Even if no one around is aware of this error in judgment, even if there is no ridicule, it is difficult to acknowledge that one has totally missed.

If we apply any of the above to the handcrafter who offers his work for sale, we see that it comes out this way:

1. If no one will buy your work (especially while others are selling well), you just cannot help but feel that people who pass your booth are laughing at you. To make matters worse, it isn't at all unusual to have someone make "smart" comments. If you are selling everything in sight, smart remarks fly right over your head. But if this is the second day of the show and you have yet to make a sale, such comments are extremely frustrating.

2. An even worse situation is when someone in authority shows that your work is not appreciated. Perhaps the screening committee for the art festival rejected your work. So the committee is made up largely of volunteers who know little or nothing about the craft in question . . . still, they *are* the committee and they *did* reject your work. One cannot rationalize your way out of this happily. A similar but even more difficult situation arises when a recognized authority rejects your work yet accepts work in the same category from someone whose work just does not seem as good as yours. The above situations are not all conjured up out of my imagination; I have known similar episodes to occur several times in the judging for any large festival. Undoubtedly they always will.

3. In conclusion, there comes a time when, if your work is similar to that of another handcrafter and priced about the same, it is difficult not to feel

frustrated and irritated at yourself and the world when his work sells and yours doesn't.

We can sum up by noting that the beginning craftsperson who offers his work for sale is likely to get into situations where he can lose face. That is always painful. Now you have been warned! Such experiences are inevitable in the commercial marketplace. At least you know now that when it does happen, it is not unique. In fact, you will be exceptional if something like this does not happen.

It is interesting to realize also that the hobbyist who is successful in his professional career is far more vulnerable than one whose success is modest. No matter what we say, most of us measure success in terms of dollars. I have found that the rule works like this: The more money one makes in commerce, the more difficult it seems to offer one's handcrafts for sale. Exceptions to this rule must exist, but they are few. Perhaps you have heard of the jewelry by Picasso? Some very expensive pieces, fabulous items whose fabrication required remarkable craftsmanship. The fact is that Picasso did not make a single one of those pieces. Experienced craftsmen executed his design. Thus to speak of Picasso as a jeweler is quite misleading. Speak of him as a jewelry designer, yes. But not as a jeweler! Picasso already had plenty of self-confidence in his work as an artist, and he didn't expose himself to loss of face by designing jewelry. Had he attempted to fabricate even one of his pieces it might have been far different.

The rule stated above was that the more successful one is in his profession, the more difficult it is for him to exhibit his craft products for sale. Picasso's jewelry is not an exception to this rule because he was not offering work of his own craftsmanship for sale. Most apparent exceptions to the stated rule really are not exceptions at all.

If it is true that the more successful one is at

his profession the more difficult it is for him to exhibit his craft products for sale, it is also true that the less successful one is in a professional career, the easier it is for him to exhibit his work for sale. He who has nothing to lose has nothing to fear. One sees the most amazing hodgepodges at festivals—often selling briskly.

Now for self-analysis. You have been reluctant to offer your craft work for sale. You have given all sorts of reasons for this . . . reasons that appear fundamentally sound. But in light of what has been said in this chapter, take another look. What are the *real* reasons? No one else can possibly know, so be honest with yourself, try not to rationalize your actions. If you are reluctant to display your work, (admit this to yourself. Whatever the reason or reasons,) bring them out into the light of day and admit them. Once you have done this they will become less important.

Sometimes a personal example is the best illustration, so here goes. I had reached the executive level in the aerospace industry but wanted to sell my own handcrafted jewelry. As a matter of fact, I found myself in the situation of *having* to sell because the house was brimming over with the stuff. How to get started? How to find out whether I was producing anything good enough to sell?

An obvious answer was right at hand. The Pacific Northwest abounds in local art festivals all summer. Enter one of those, set up a stall and have a go at it. But it wasn't quite that simple. The closest festival had disadvantages:

    1. A committee screened entries and accepted or rejected the applicant;

    2. The show was just too close to home. People would know me. A lot of associates would walk by my stall. How would they react?

The fact is, I just couldn't do it. Just didn't have the nerve to enter that local art festival. The possibility of loss of face was too great. Through cautious inquiries I discovered an art festival a hundred miles away. It seemed a logical possibility. They did not screen—just charged an entrance fee. It seemed made to order. The chance of associates going by my booth was remote. The danger of losing face was minimum. Eventually I would have to face exposing my work to the public. Why not now?

After the festival I added up the score. Though my ego was bruised and battered, the positive results outweighed the negative. Things had sold and at a reasonable price. By this, I mean that my costs were absorbed, an important point that I cover in depth later. All this to the good. On the minus side, I had discovered that I did not know how to cope with the inevitable smart remarks. Unfortunately, it is rare to go through any art festival without getting some of this. In the beginning it can be hard to ignore. Teenagers have an uncanny ability to say things that can be overlooked only by someone with plenty of self-confidence. Beginners have to build their resistance from scratch.

After the shot of confidence generated by this successful experience, it was not all that difficult to enter the local festival the next year. As you might have guessed, my work passed the committee's screening. This local festival draws a large following, a buying crowd. I soon established a sales pattern of over several thousand dollars' worth of handcrafted jewelry in the two and one half days of this important local show. Obviously, those old fears had no basis in reality.

Then came the year that the committee rejected my work. Certainly the committee had their reasons . . . perhaps they were seeking variety that year. Whatever it was, the rejection still hurt. It hurt somewhat less because a success pattern had been established. The fact that a local painter was rejected at the same time made it a bit easier. The rejected painter normally did considerably more dollar volume of business in that festival than I did.

One runs across all sorts of problems. A friend of mine found herself in a predicament caused entirely by the rules set up by another committee. This friend does exceptionally fine bronze figures and has become rather well known. When she was invited to an important festival out of the immediate area, the artist decided to go, in spite of the fact that it was for five days, ten hours daily. It turned out to be a slow show. Lots of lookers and no buyers. That gets old quickly. After several days, each of ten hours, it gets *very* old.

However, someone became interested in an expensive bronze. The price would cover the bills for the trip and the five days' time spent at the show. This affluent patron of the arts offered his check, but the committee—there has to be a committee in this yarn, of course—did not want a check. They wanted good hard cash. The would-be purchaser offered a credit card. The committee held out for cash.

You can imagine the state of mind of the artist. It would not bother her to take a check. But the committee, who was working on a percentage of the sales, did not look at it that way. Finally, the committee chairman took my friend aside, "Let's just say this never happened. We don't know anything about it." And the chairman left.

The embarrassed artist accepted the check without question. No doubt she was right, for it did not bounce. Of course, it might have turned out that the committee was correct. All businesses have a certain percentage of bad checks. But that's not the point. The decision should never have been a committee function, it should have been left to the artist.

No one answer is right for all situations at all

times. And no committee in existence has the right answer always. Count yourself fortunate if the committees with which you deal have some right answers once in a while.

To sum up, when you begin exhibiting in public, you can anticipate some unpleasant experiences. Decisions that hurt are to be expected. Some of the people who attend the festivals will make disparaging remarks.

Whether or not you have exhibited yet, you must have met people like the one in the following personal experience. A spectator started in at the very first booth with, "My three-year-old grandchild can do better work than that." At the next booth this type of remark was repeated. (I have noticed that such comments are seldom addressed to the craftsman, usually to someone with the outspoken spectator. But always loudly enough to make certain that the exhibitor doesn't get left out of the action.) At the third and fourth booths it was the same.

However, the festival chairman had been in the group at the first booth, and he had trailed the speaker to the others. Finally, he tapped the spectator on the shoulder and said, loudly enough to be heard by the entire group, "Pardon me, my name is _____, chairman of the exhibits this year. Since it's obvious you have so much talent, we'd like to invite you to take part in the festival next year. How many booths would you like to have?"

While this hardly seemed to dent the ego of the spectator, it certainly was good for the participating craftsmen!

So take the pulse of your ego. Confront the possibility of losing face. If the threat is severe, find a way to minimize it. Make a dry run around the problem. Begin in a situation that has minimum danger. It is easiest to get started where no one knows you.

Today there are art festivals everywhere.

Look at a few of the craft magazines for some idea of what's going on. In many cases, you can be assured of a place in a festival by payment of a small fee.

If you are really up tight about putting your crafts before the public and cannot even face an out-of-town festival, you may be able to find someone to take your work for you. On a percentage basis, naturally. In this case, the risk is absolutely minimal. Scout around. There will almost always be someone going to that festival. If the festival is a bust and you don't sell a single item, it didn't cost you much either. Go around the problem if you just can't get over it. One of these days, you will realize that you no longer have a problem. Now you have passed one of the major hurdles.

Now we come to the question of attitude and situations where you can learn from others. Whereas experience only can teach one how to handle festival committees and the buying public, it is good to realize one can learn more than a craft when taking a class. Obviously, it is possible to learn craft skills from books and to accomplish fine work without classes, but if it is at all possible, join a class. Learn from the students who work with you. Each will have a different attitude toward his work. One of the important benefits from being part of a handcraft class is the contact with other students. You can compare your work with what is being done by others who have a similar amount of training. This is especially true if you happen to be a perfectionist, and it seems that many handcrafters *do* have such a tendency. However, while this drive for perfection is necessary to attain fine work, in the beginning learning should be placed before the concern over perfection.

Perfection in handwork is not easily attained. It takes time, lots of time, before one has the skill. Slight imperfections are characteristic of hand-crafted work. This does not mean one is deliberately sloppy, rather that one does not always take the time and effort to erase these imperfections.

Once again, I am basing my statements on personal experience. After my wife and I had spent several thousand hours learning how to fabricate metals for jewelry, we took a week-long course one summer with Ruth Pennington, who was then teaching jewelry making at the University of Washington. We took Ruth samples of our work and pointed out the imperfections, of which we were all too aware. Ruth looked these pieces over and commented that the work was good. Then she said, "Your work is not supposed to look machine-made. Let the mark of the craftsman show now and then so that there is no question that it is hand-made."

By the end of the week, the idea that the mark of the craftsman may show had been fairly well drilled into my mind. A few months later came the first important commission: a pair of earrings, jade set in gold. Naturally, that work was done very carefully, no solder seams, no irregularities. Each earring was a mirror opposite of the other. The work was literally perfect and was delivered to the customer with considerable pride.

Imagine my chagrin when the earrings were rejected. "I don't like them. They look like what I asked for, yes, but they could have been made by a machine. They just don't look like one-of-a-kind originals to me," the customer explained.

That finally did it. What Ruth Pennington had said really got through this time. I am stressing the need to understand the difference between handcrafted work and machine-made items because beginners frequently have a negative or defensive attitude about their work. This sort of attitude can unfortunately carry over when the time comes for that first sale. Your frame of mind when you approach potential customers can determine the outcome. If anything negative exists in your approach, then you are not ready to sell.

I am sure you have noticed craft students who can speak only negatively of their work. "It just didn't turn out the way I planned it." You can admire and compliment the item, but the pessimistic student is not easily moved. "You see something I do not see. There's no way I can be pleased with something like this that didn't turn out right." Who would believe you could learn from such a situation? But you can, and it is vital that you develop a positive attitude. It takes time, lots of time, before one gains skill, and if you view those first efforts in the right frame of mind, then so will potential buyers.

By the time my wife and I got around to teaching jewelry-making classes, the importance of the right attitude had become second nature to us. Thus we stressed it from the very beginning. However, it took us several years of teaching and helping students get started in selling their work before a definite approach to making the first sale evolved. In discussing classes with a potential student, the first indoctrination took place. "We expect students to sell their work. Sooner or later you must either begin selling or stop producing. So the best way to start is with the willingness to sell what you make from the very first completed item."

Our students understood that they were expected to complete a jewelry item each lesson, beginning with the first. Lesson one gave techniques required to make a silver band ring, of stamped design, from sheet sterling. The finished ring was polished and antiquing was optional. Since many students had never used a torch, the solder joint was the big hurdle. But before we got into techniques, it was emphasized to the class that invisible solder joints are extremely difficult and hardly expected in the first item made by hand. Such skill comes only after considerable time has been spent in the fabrication of metals.

Thus no student was surprised to find that his solder joint showed. The design—which came from handmade stamping tools—was always unique. Thus it was virtually impossible for any two students to produce similar work.

So as part of the comments at the beginning of the class, it became routine to open with something like this, "This is your first lesson but you will complete a sterling band ring this session. It will be an original design, good enough for you to sell at a fair price ... provided you follow these suggestions."

We would also tell the same class, "Handmade work isn't expected to be perfect. If what you create looks machine-made, there is no point in handcrafts. You must learn from the beginning to leave the mark of the craftsman on your work. The imperfections are the very things that make your work unique.

"Take your finished work from this first class and show it with pride. Take it to work with you and wherever there are several people around, show it off. 'Look what I made last night.' Most of those who see your work will admire it and comment that they wish they could do something like that.

"Be prepared for someone to ask, 'Will you sell it to me. How much is it?' Quick as a flash you will answer, 'You won't get it cheap! It's my very first finished piece and I like it.' Then ignore the question, go on as if it had never been asked. If the questioner really wants to buy, he will not let the matter drop. He will come to you later. Then give him a price. One that you had worked out previously. Your potential buyer can take it or leave it. It's just that simple. If he says, 'Yes,' you have made your first sale.

"Suppose on the other hand, you take that item

to the office and show it off and someone asks, 'What will you take for it?' You reply, 'Well, it's really my first finished piece. The teacher helped me a lot with it. It just didn't come out quite the way I had planned it. I hope that I can do better work when I have had more time in the class. I really don't know what it's worth.'

"You guessed it. No sale. Your own negative feelings have been expressed and they will always kill any chance for someone to be captivated by the item. Remember—when you show your first piece of completed work you are not doing this in order to make a sale. You are prepared to sell if the situation is right, but that is not the reason for displaying the piece. You have created something with your own hands. It is yours and thus unique. You therefore have every right to be proud of it—you have developed the roots of a positive attitude."

2

Pricing Your Products

The problems facing the craftsman who wishes to start selling his work are many. It is not easy to find someone with the right background to give advice on selling handcrafts.

The majority of those who teach handcrafts in the educational system are semiprofessional craftsmen. That is to say, they may be well trained in art and the skill of teaching but have limited experience in selling their own handcrafts. If we assume that their production is small, it is likely that any work they do offer for sale will be in a special situation: one in which their status as a teacher may well influence the potential buyer. Thus it is rare that the teacher in the educational system can be of assistance to someone who wants to start selling his crafts.

It is much the same with the usual retailer of craft products. Most of the time, he is a professional salesman. It is not at all unusual to find that he has no experience whatever in creating with his hands.

Thus it is the professional craftsman who is most likely to be able to offer sound guidance to the beginner who wants to start selling his work. It is usually the case that such a person's experience will be helpful even if he is in a totally different craft field. The factors involved are very much the same for all handcrafts.

It is absolutely essential that your products are priced correctly. It is very easy to aim too low or too high. An established price structure is difficult to change. That does not mean that the changes necessary for cost increases in materials cannot be made; rather it means that it is extremely difficult to double or treble prices because they were too low initially. Real thought must be given to price structure before going into the marketplace. Pricing is not simple, and you will never make a more important decision.

It is well worth the time and effort to understand fully just what is involved in pricing before you begin selling. A brief look at the system by which most products are marketed in the United States is enlightening. The average product goes through a whole chain of marketing organizations before getting to the retail customer. Obviously, each link in the chain adds cost to the final price.

The producer (handcrafter or manufacturer) can choose to sell his product himself—by one of several methods—or to use a distribution system. While there are various levels of distributors, for our purposes we are discussing a marketing organization able to sell the products to wholesalers or retailers, or directly to retail customers—or any combination of these methods.

While it is fairly obvious that the various steps in the marketing each add to the cost of the item, people often make the mistake of thinking that direct sales do not add to the price of the item.

A typical situation can be illustrated by the plight of a craftsman who produces candles. His cost is $1 each. He feels that a markup of 35 percent will pay for his labor profitably. Thus his candles are priced at $1.35 each. He honestly thinks that he has done a good job of pricing. In fact, the whole arrangement seems great. He produces and sells a lot of candles from his home workshop. As business volume increases, however, he realizes that he is spending so much time ringing up sales that he is not producing many candles. If he hires someone to handle sales, his costs will certainly increase. If he continues to cope with it himself then his production will go down. At about that time, he realizes that he has not based his prices correctly.

Of course, if our candle craftsman discovered that he did not have customers coming to his home workshop, he might consider that the local art festival would be the place to sell his production. Upon reading the entry requirements, however, he learns to his dismay that the festival charges a nominal fee for registration, as well as taking a commission of 30 percent on all items sold at the fair. In addition, the craftsman has to consider the setting up and dismantling of the booth, transport to and from the show, and breakage as well as his time attending the festival—time that he might have spent producing candles.

Any price increase that this craftsman considers will not be nominal. Will the radical change in prices mean that his candles are so expensive that no one will buy them? At this point, the craftsman wonders how he went so far astray in his pricing. Unfortunately, he started at the wrong point, and many of his assumptions were incorrect. His original retail price (cost + labor) was completely unreal. If the purpose of selling your handcraft is to enable you to become self-supporting, it is vital that you clarify the hidden costs.

The following list was compiled with the help of information from the Small Business and Loans Administration. Branches of this government agency are located throughout the country. Basic cost considerations are detailed as:

1. Costs of materials, labor, and overhead of premises;
2. Selling expenses, including delivery;
3. General administrative expenses, including office help;
4. Profit.

When businessmen are asked about their profit percentage, they invariably have the following reply: "If I place my money in a savings bank, it will earn a fixed percentage of interest. I will have no worries and no work. Each quarter the savings bank adds interest to my money." In the seventies, the average rate of interest paid by savings banks on money in savings accounts has been 5 percent. Thus, a business's profit margin should certainly be higher than that to justify the work and risk.

If you use the above list, you are able to estimate 1, 3, and 4 from your own figures. You know what your materials cost you. You can run a time check on yourself (more on that later) and, when you have decided on a rate of pay, your salary is established. The tax laws specify what tax deductions can be made for businesses operating from private residences—what portion of the rent or mortgage and what portion of telephone and utilities can be deducted. An accountant can swiftly itemize these costs if you do not handle your own taxes.

Item 2 contains the pitfalls for the unwary. However you choose to sell your product, you must clarify the costs involved. Your product can go from you through all five links of the marketing chain:

Craftsman to distributor to wholesaler to retailer to retail customer.

If you choose to follow the above, then the following percentage markups are average:

The craftsman (combining 1, 2, 3, and 4) arrives at	$1.00
The distributor adds 35 percent	$1.35
The wholesaler adds 45 percent	$1.96
The retailer adds 100 percent	$3.92

Frequently, the retail percentage is called 50 percent. It might be less confusing if we put it another way: the retail markup is never less than double the wholesale price.

While the retailer is often accused of charging high prices, he often has more marketing cost than either the distributor or wholesaler.

Often, the first reaction to the above pricing structure is outrage at the way the cost is escalated. Then, the craftsman thinks, "If I sidestep one of the links in the marketing chain I can save money." That person has fallen into one of the pitfalls that trap many. If you sell to a distributor, you have to learn his business methods. If you go directly to a wholesaler, you are taking on the salesman's job; besides, the distributor's methods will differ from those of the wholesaler. Who will pay you for your time spent in learning new conditions and selling to different links in the marketing chain?

Perhaps you are able to go directly to retail outlets. Again, the selling conditions are different (see Chapter 6). Whatever method of distribution you prefer, each has its own costs. Your cost in contacting the distributor—whether he is at step 1 or 3 in the marketing organization—must always be included in your analysis of expenses.

Now that we have defined the structure of pricing, we should clarify several basic points. First, and of major importance, the craftsman must determine what dollar per hour rate he is willing to work for. If he is willing to work for 25¢ an hour, that's his business. However, he must establish an hourly rate for himself. Once he has done this, he must refuse to work at a lower wage. For the sake of comparison, let's look at the nationally established minimum wage. Of course, while it keeps creeping higher, it does represent the lowest pay rate for the least skilled worker. The unskilled beginner gets the minimum wage regardless of his capability, production rate, or the number of mistakes he may make in the course of an average day. The craftsman who accepts a rate below the established minimum wage seems to be indicating that he places little value on his own work and skill. Does this indicate a positive attitude? It seems reasonable that the skilled craftsman would be paid a rate at least double that of the minimum wage.

Now to arrive at a formula by which the craftsman can price his creations. Let the letter L stand for labor cost. The time required to produce any item on a unit basis is expressed by the letter T; it may be a fraction of an hour or many hours. The formula $L \times T$ equals the labor cost for any item produced.

Example: One establishes a minimum wage of $3.50 an hour. It takes 15 minutes (0.25 hour) to make a hand-dipped candle. The labor cost of the candle is:

$$\$3.50 \times 0.25 = \$.875$$

Please do not leave off that final 5—the figure above is not $.87, it is $.875.

The letter M represents cost of materials. This varies from one craft to another. In some cases, M is so low it seems of little importance. When costly materials are used, however, M can be more important than L. M is often directly related to how the producing craftsman obtains what he needs (see Chapter 3). This part of the cost is very important in the analysis required in pricing products. A craftsman may use items which cost nothing directly; perhaps they are found on the beach, for example. In that case, cost of materials M is not zero but is determined by how many units he finds per hour, at his regular hourly rate of pay.

Example: The candle craftsman collects beach stones to embed in his candles. On the average, he picks up thirty such stones each hour. It takes an hour each way to and from the beach. What is M, the unit cost of his beach stones?

Three hours on the beach @ $3.50 per hour	$10.50
Two hours driving time @ $3.50 per hour	7.00
Gasoline, mileage, both ways	10.00
Total	$27.50

M, the unit cost for the beach stones, is thus established for this trip at $27.50 divided by 90 (the number collected). The beach stones which supposedly cost nothing have really cost the craftsman $.305 each.

However, the candle craftsman has forgotten yet a further part of the pricing formula: Overhead. This is a somewhat mysterious term to most craftsmen. It is full of uncertainties. Overhead is the total of all costs other than direct labor and materials. Overhead covers tools, bulk supplies, paper, pencils, electricity, heat, water, telephone, and the work area in which the craftsman produces the things he sells. Everything not directly part of the production process is properly called overhead. Training, the time spent in ordering supplies, time spent on designing, time spent in talking to customers or potential buyers—all of this is hidden cost and in total is O for overhead.

Now our formula is:

$$L + M + O = \text{Wholesale Price}$$

If you come up with any other answer then you are wrong. And, as we have mentioned earlier, R—the retail price—for handcrafts is generally not less than double the wholesale price.

$$R = W \times 2 \text{ (minimum)}$$

Now let's put some numbers into the formula and make some use of it. If the candle craftsman produces 4 pieces per hour, at his self-established hourly rate of \$3.50, his labor (L) is \$.875 per unit. If we use M (cost of materials) of \$.305 from our arithmetic on the unit cost of the beach stones, we have two of the three costs required to compute the wholesale price. Overhead, O, the hidden costs are not quite so easy to compute.

In the beginning, there is simply no way it can be done accurately and in the detail needed to compute O for a candle. The only way to obtain fairly meaningful data is to take an arbitrary definition of O and use that for the time being.

So long as there are no people on the payroll and all the work is handled by the craftsman himself, the rule of thumb for overhead is that O is a third of either L or M, whichever is higher. (If there is even one person on the payroll, the rule of thumb is that O is equal to a third of L plus M.)

For our purposes, we will say that the craftsman is producing the candles himself. This means that O is established (as in the above formula) as a third of either L or M, whichever is higher. In this case, L is higher at \$.875 per unit. O for this illustration becomes a third of L (.333 $\times$ .875) or .291 per unit.

Thus the pricing of the hand dipped candles becomes:

$$L + M + O = W \text{ (wholesale)}$$
$$\$.875 + \$.305 + \$.291 = \$1.47 \text{ per unit}$$

If the retail price is wholesale times two, $1.47 × 2 = $2.94 per unit—or candle. That figure is a long way from where the craftsman first established his selling price at $1.35.

At this point, the bewildered craftsman explodes, "Nobody in his right mind is going to pay $2.94 for my candles. What can I do?"

Well, Mr. Craftsman, you do have a problem and you will have to make a decision. You can establish your price at $2.94 per candle and hold it there, or you can discontinue the item. Perhaps, however, you can find a way to reduce the costs. Those are the only alternatives, and we will look at the possibilities in depth before making that final decision.

In the first place, the craftsman does not know whether anyone will pay $2.94 for one of his candles until they are put out for sale at that price. We craftsmen are frequently guilty of so seriously underpricing our work that the buying public gets the impression that it isn't worth much. It is just as easy to lose sales from underpricing as from overpricing. It is impossible to know what people will pay for a product until it is exposed to public view with a clear price tag.

Perhaps the candle craftsman considers the time when he was selling his wares from his home studio with little time and effort involved in the process. He wonders if by selling at the established retail price of $2.94 he is making an extra profit. However, he should realize that the additional money was earned because he took over the function of the retail salesman. During that selling period, he was unable to function as a craftsman.

Occasionally, you may choose to copy the retail shops' selling method of putting merchandise out at bargain prices, for a limited period. Certainly that is your right but do keep in mind that this is not changing the established retail price, it is offering a special bargain.

If you ignore the realities of this pricing formula, you will never learn to price your products and—perhaps more importantly—it will be virtually impossible for you to become self-supporting as a craftsman. You may choose to produce without having made such an analysis. Or you may choose to work for $.25 an hour. That is your business. Can you, however, live on the income you earn in this way?

To sum up, it is essential that you analyze your costs and establish a minimum wage rate. If you find that you are not earning this amount, find out what is wrong and do something about it. Either discontinue the item or find some way to make it pay off for you.

If you are selling at a loss, there is no way to improve the situation by selling in greater quantity. Chapter 3 goes into the details of how to study your creations and possibly turn a loser into a winner.

3

Constantly Reevaluate Your Work

The individual who wishes to become self-supporting through the sale of his work needs to evaluate his work regularly. One should keep an eye on two things: (1) How can the product be improved? (2) How can costs be reduced (thus increasing profit)?

Item (1) Product Improvement. By using more costly materials than those in the original, it is possible to upgrade an item and sell it profitably. The American consumer has definite ideas. If an item appears low in price, he just won't buy. He is just as quick to reject an article on the basis of low price as he is to turn down that which is overpriced. Teenagers—whose buying power represents a large part of the market—are especially discriminating in this respect; they certainly look items over before making the buying decision. You must also consider the consumers' attitudes—if the buying public considers something is junk, such a product will not sell regardless of the intrinsic merit of the creation.

One of the best ways to illustrate this is with an actual case history. My wife and I know a highly skilled craftsman whose work is intricate and beautiful. Her creations show not only real skill but great imagination. But in order to sell, her prices are very, very low. You see, she turns tin cans into art objects. The American consumer considers tin cans junk and is unlikely to pay top prices. That small percentage, the jet setters, might. But your average citizen is not about to pay for something he considers garbage. This tendency must be taken into consideration by the craftsman. If this artist created the very same designs in sterling silver of the same gauge as the tin cans, she might be able to sell her entire production at top prices. Even at the present price of silver! That is the kind of world we live in and it cannot be overlooked or ignored.

In the early days of my career as a jewelry designer and craftsman, I was fascinated to discover that there are two kinds of jade: nephrite and jadeite. They differ chemically but both are true jade. Fine and very costly nephrite is sold in Wyoming, Alaska, and British Columbia. However, in the Seattle area, nephrite is a dead item. On the other hand, jadeite, the so-called Oriental jade, sells well in Seattle.

What's behind this? Well, nephrite is mined in Wyoming, Alaska, and British Columbia. Undoubtedly, the potential jade buyer, usually the tourist, has the idea that one of these days he will go to Wyoming (or Alaska or British Columbia) and discover himself a fine piece of jade.

The Seattle jewelry craftsman who finds that he cannot sell nephrite items could replace them with jadeite and probably sell the latter readily.

This example serves to illustrate the way one

can change a product so that the buying public will feel that it has been upgraded.

We know another person in the crafts who has been painting weeds and seeds for more years than most of us have been handcrafters. She has had no problem selling anything she ever produced. But this artist is always taking another look at her work to see what can be done for additional product appeal. At a recent art festival, Betty's familiar weed and seed paintings had taken on a new look . . . the vase in which the foliage was contained had an Oriental look. Of all things, there was an Oriental signature next to the frame. Betty readily confessed that she had learned to draw the Japanese characters for her name. These pictures were going as fast as she could paint them. Here the product change—or improvement—relates to consumer appeal rather than to materials used.

Of course, it is a good idea to keep yourself as well informed as possible about the buying public's mood. Trends are inexplicable.

All at once something is "in" and is very hot. For no apparent reason. You cannot produce enough of them. In the late sixties, large pendants and handmade chains sold almost before they were finished. Then, practically overnight, they were out. You could hardly give them away.

It is impossible to outguess the buying trends. But you can be sure of one thing. It isn't enough to rely on the fashion magazines. They are right about as often as the weatherman.

If it does not appear practical to upgrade your work by using better or different materials or new designs, it is necessary to consider cost reduction, Item (2). This can be accomplished either (a) by lowering the cost of materials, or (b) by reducing the cost (time) of labor.

There was a time in this country when the industrial efficiency expert made enemies wherever he went because a stopwatch was always in his hand. He was an expert in time and motion studies, always telling people how they could speed up their work. So most of us are likely to back off when confronted with the idea that we should keep one eye on the clock . . . even if it is for a short period. Much of the time, the craftsman has not the slightest idea how long the entire project took, let alone the time spent on the individual steps involved.

I watch time expended very closely, mostly for one reason: I want to do so many, many other things that it seems foolish to waste time. Why do something the wrong way when it could be done more quickly and easily the right way? I can burn up hours and hours of what could have been productive work time chasing some idea that just came across . . . and not even feel the least guilty about it. But if it takes twice as long as it should to make a simple jewelry repair, I feel quite frustrated—I consider that time wasted. The dedicated craftsman never has enough time. With these thoughts in mind, we take a look at how the craftsman uses the stopwatch constructively. Do remember that this is an exercise of short duration. Eventually you will be able to estimate your time quite accurately and swiftly.

In order to know how long it takes to make an item:

   1. Break the project into simple, logical steps;
   2. Work on 6–12 items, recording the time required in each item for each step.

Does anything look out of line with the sequence? Perhaps a finished item, made in four steps, required 20 minutes. If you find that step 3 took half the total time, start looking there. You may even find, after analysis, that work time was good on that long stretch, step 3. You may also compare it with the other steps and wonder what in the world you were doing all that time.

In an effort to increase your efficiency, rework the problem area step and watch yourself go about it. How far do you have to move your hands? Do your hands cross over each other? Is it necessary to hunt for a special tool?

After this study, place each tool and component used so that you require a minimum of movement or changing of things from one hand to the other. Each time you put something down and pick up something else, it costs you time. So lay out your work area so that movement is at a minimum, then check your time again. In many cases, after checking tool placement, sequence of movements, etc., a reduction of as much as 50 percent in work time can be accomplished.

Even after you have done everything possible to work efficiently (lazily!), an item may not be economical to produce. Then the question arises: Can the actual process be changed in order to reduce time? For instance, a twisted wire loop may be just as acceptable to the buying public as a beautifully soldered joint. Try changing techniques and see how the public responds before you make a final decision.

If you are creative, an infinite number of design possibilities are possible, and there is no way to run an efficiency analysis on all of them. Think of whatever project you are doing in terms of work units. The simplest operation in what you are making represents a time unit.

Once again, I will illustrate a general principle by using the familiar techniques of my craft, jewelry. Several steps are required to make a simple loop earring. Perhaps the simplest step (work unit) is the bending of the wire around a mandrel. Cutting each loop may also be a work unit. A more complex step, soldering the loop, may take twice as long as the simple steps. Thus, soldering becomes a two-unit operation. Finishing, polishing, washing, and drying can easily take three or four times as long as the simplest steps, and thus become three or four-unit operations.

Time your simplest work step—the single work unit procedure—and give this a value based on your hourly rate. For more complex steps, multiply the unit time by the value of the single unit.

Suppose the simplest operation takes one minute. At your self-established hourly wage of $3 the one minute step (single work unit) has a value or cost of 5 cents. Sixty single units @ 5 cents = $3 an hour. More complex units, those of three, five, or ten-unit operations are multiplied by the single unit rate (5 cents) and become 15, 25, or 50 cents respectively.

In the end you learn to compare time spent on any work technique with the single work unit and before long can readily estimate how much that costs in production time. In the process, you also analyze how work can be done with greater ease or speed.

Few craftsmen enjoy the repetition involved in a production run. It is difficult to exercise the self-discipline necessary to go through the process outlined in this chapter. But it is virtually impossible to arrive at efficient techniques without such analysis. It does pay off. Once you have done some production line work and sold it, you are ready to produce individual pieces efficiently. Consider the grinding out of production work a self-imposed apprenticeship necessary as preparation for better things.

Item (2)—how can costs be reduced—should also be applied to your buying. Important cost reductions can be accomplished through wholesale and quantity buying of your raw materials. These are totally different procedures. Even when one buys wholesale, further savings can be effected by quantity purchases.

In order to buy wholesale, you need evidence that you are engaged in retail selling. Often, a sales tax license is adequate. Such licenses can be obtained from your state department of taxes and frequently they are issued free or for a nominal sum. Occasionally, a supplier will require additional information but often, if there is any problem, a purchase order on your letterhead will be sufficient to convince the supplier of your validity as a wholesale buyer.

It is important to note, also, that the sales tax license exempts you from paying sales tax when you buy materials—since you will be reselling the end product and tax will be paid on that. Most states have reciprocity with other states over use of sales tax licenses.

However, even though you buy wholesale, that alone is not assurance that you are getting the most reasonable price. There is a tremendous variation in price range for many items used by craftsmen. An almost identical tool may have four different prices from four suppliers—and there may be quite a spread between those prices. This also applies to many materials.

It is therefore essential to read the publications for your field and write for catalogs. Not just one or two of them but all that are available. Even if you never buy from that supplier, it is often worth the modest cost just to learn where not to buy.

Compare prices and quality. Order a small quantity for trial. In most cases, each supply house prices similar items differently, so buy one item from Chicago, others from Los Angeles, some from New York, etc., in order to get the most from your dollar. The practice of buying almost everything from one supplier is generally more costly.

4

Selling From Your Home Studio

Rarely can a craftsman produce enough by his own efforts initially to justify a retail shop. Even when he has his own shop someone is needed to take care of it, for one cannot sell and produce simultaneously. Certainly, the retail shop is not the answer for most selling craftsmen, at least in the beginning.

Perhaps the best solution to the problem of where to sell your handcrafts is to set aside part of your own home as a studio. The word studio is very important here. The natural thing one thinks of with studio is "artist." Perhaps you do not see yourself as an artist? All too frequently, people quibble over the meaning of a word. The dictionary's definition of studio is "a room or place in which some form of art is pursued." This reference includes artists and photographers, as well as radio, television, and movie work. If you have the initiative, self-confidence, and self-discipline to attempt to become a self-supporting craftsman, then certainly you can name a corner of your front room, basement, or garage your studio.

When my wife and I were contemplating entering the field of handcrafted jewelry full time, we felt it best to move to the city. We sold our suburban home, and the mortgage was switched to the new address in town. In order to operate with any degree of ease, a business license was essential. However, our new home was just out of the business zone. Traditionally, our city officials were not tolerant of commercial enterprises in residential zones. We therefore duly applied for a business license for Studio 714—the number of the house —in the name of Garrison and Garrison, artists in several media.

There was never any question. The business license was issued as requested and has been renewed annually ever since. But because our home was clearly out of the business zone, the thought of outside advertising was totally out. Yet who could quarrel with an attractive hand-carved wooden sign in the yard that read simply, Seven-fourteen?

So do not overlook the potential value of that word studio. It conveys an impression but still is not definite enough to pin you down. Everyone expects a studio to somehow produce work that will in some way be offered for sale, but there is no one way to tell just what might be produced in a studio. Take advantage of the vagueness of the term and make the most of it . . . your studio can be just about anything you want it to be.

Now that you have a studio, you should get business cards printed. If possible, the card should emphasize art. As the head of the concern, you are the president, manager, and creative product designer. But your clients are most interested in the merchandise, so let your card be clear. Many people will ask for your card, and they are not just being polite. They really want to tuck it away so that when and if they wish to buy from you they can locate your studio. Such cards need not be costly; today no one is impressed with engraved business cards. Just keep the card from being busy—cluttered with too much information. The opportunity for people to pick up your card at art festivals may be more important to you in the long run than the amount of work sold during those shows.

Nothing is wrong with a colorful card. Go as "far out" as you like in this respect. Just keep it relatively simple. Let your card tell people what you do, your basic field, and where to find you. The rest will take care of itself.

Studio established, business cards printed, you are ready to think about other forms of advertising. Here the best policy is to keep the tone of the advertising in line with the idea that you are operating a home studio. A small, regular classified advertisement in the local newspaper may generate a good amount of work. Television spots are relatively expensive. Another way to advertise what you are doing is to encourage publicity. Any kind of publicity (within reason!) is good publicity. Accept *any* invitation that is extended for you to speak to a group or demonstrate your work and let people know what you are doing.

Here again, it is attitude that counts. If you go out and try to generate publicity, it is likely to fail. If you have the right frame of mind to accept it when it is offered, there may be no end to your chances to let people know what you are doing. The staff writers for your local paper are always seeking fresh material, and if you are approached, do not hesitate to let it be known that you will be glad to cooperate. Brief articles in the local paper are quite useful publicity.

Groups that meet regularly are especially good possibilities for talks and demonstrations. The program chairman who has to find fifty-two programs during his term in office can get awfully desperate. He reaches the point where he'll gladly settle for anything that isn't a rerun of what he gave the troops last week. That's where you may come in. Just let it be known that you are available. Far more often than you would believe, there will be opportunities to place your story before some of the people in the community.

Of all the discreet methods by which you may get publicity, by far the best is that of teaching. Announce that you will take a class of beginners in the handcraft of your choice, and you will find this opens all sorts of doors. Today there are always more people wanting to take classes than there are teachers. Your students will become your best advertisement. They *will* talk about you and your classes and your work. Because they are proud of what they have accomplished they are necessarily proud of you, their teacher. So what they say is said with the right attitude—a very positive affirmation that nothing but good can come from what you are doing.

You may not feel qualified to teach. However, if you have gained a reasonable, perhaps even a high, degree of skill in techniques which are not known to the would-be students, then you can teach them something—not everything you wish you could teach, or not everything the student wishes to learn. But you can give them something they do not have: personal contact with someone who has acquired skills and techniques in the field of interest.

Teaching is not necessarily formal. There may be no classroom or formal class period or even fees involved. Someone may simply say, "Would you let me come by some time when you could show me something of what you are doing?" When you say, "Yes," you have become a teacher. The very first time you take up your tools and say to someone,

"This is the way I do it," you have become a teacher.

Perhaps the most informal of all teaching situations is that in which you are at the local art festival, "demonstrating" during the time of the show. People will watch and they will ask questions. At that point you have become a teacher. In a limited way, yes. Informal, yes. Still, you have become a teacher. And if you can teach a bit in the hub-bub of what goes on during the art festival, surely you can help a beginner who wants to just drop by and spend some time seeing how you get things done.

Definite classes, involving a stated time and planned requirements, come naturally after the informal teaching already described. Regardless of how good natured you are, how willing you are to share what you have learned, formal classes should compensate you adequately for your time.

It is impossible to say how much space is needed for classes, how much equipment, etc. So just estimate how much space it takes for a beginner student and when you translate this into the reality of your space situation you have determined the maximum number of students you can possibly take. Then look at the question of equipment, and tools, and you may find you have other limitations. In the end, you will conclude that you can take a certain number of students and no more.

You must also establish a definite number of lessons. I feel that it is best to limit a teaching program to a maximum of ten to twelve sessions, each no more than three hours. The beginning craftsman just cannot get much accomplished in less than three hours, no matter how good you are as a teacher. However, if a session goes beyond three hours, fatigue will set in. Perhaps it is preferable to schedule classes for around two and a half hours. Then you can let occasional sessions stretch into the three hours ... but chop them off if they threaten to go much beyond that. Few people can concentrate for such a time.

The fact that you are doing some teaching, whether formal or informal, is right in line with the use of the word studio for your handcraft activity. No one is likely to question the fact that your studio is used for teaching purposes. Artists are expected to be willing, at times, to teach others how to get started. Thus the fact that you are teaching will be right in line with the image you have created.

Naturally, precautions are necessary when you hold classes. Conform as closely as possible to the requirements of your local fire department. Regulations vary greatly in their definition of what is safe and what is unsafe. Regardless of whether or not you agree with their thinking, you must conform to the local code. If you don't, you may be shut down at any time, with little or no warning.

It is easy for someone to be hurt during classes through the use of tools, heat, chemicals, etc. There's no way to avoid possible liability if a student has an accident and chooses to sue. Perhaps the best way to lessen this potential is to clarify from the beginning that minor cuts and burns are to be expected. "You can't work with hand equipment without having it bite you once in a while." Of course, do everything reasonable to prevent even minor accidents.

You may have some coverage under liability clauses in home insurance policies. No two are alike, and the question of your activity as a handcrafting studio would require legal interpretation in your own locality.

It may well be that you should incorporate to make certain you do not incur liability. Upon incorporating, the liability shifts from the stockholder to the corporation itself. While it is true that a major liability problem might cause the corporation to collapse, it's also true at the same time that you as an individual cannot be held liable for the problems that come to the corporation to which you hold stock. That holds even if you are the sole stockholder.

The legal procedures and cost of incorporating vary greatly from state to state. In many cases, the cost is very low, if you handle the necessary paperwork rather than have an attorney. In other states, the problems of incorporation make it wise to have the services of an attorney. Check the requirements in your state. A great deal of benefit can derive from incorporation. Full responsibility rests upon the legal entity of the corporation rather than you, the individual.

5

Attending Fairs, Festivals, Carnivals, and Flea Markets

Since the late sixties, community art festivals have been sprouting all over the country. For a long time, the East Coast led, but now fairs, carnivals, and flea markets are clearly national. Perhaps the South East shows the least interest. Now there are so many shows that no one magazine can possibly detail all of them.

The nature and quality of art festivals vary so greatly that generalization is impossible. Certain factors do begin to stand out over a period of time. It is possible to predict rather accurately what is likely to happen in any given festival.

First, it is important to check how long a festival has been operating. If it has a long history, a great deal can be learned from what has happened in the past. It is also true that each such festival tends to gain momentum each year. As a general rule, the brand-new festival is not likely to attract hordes of people, whereas the festival that has been clearly established for twenty years seems to grow with each succeeding year.

One of the things you want to know before planning to participate in a festival is the way the public reacts at that particular show. Is it a "looking show" or a "buying show"? Again, the longer the festival has been established, the more likely it is to be a buying show and, also, the more likely it is to attract buyers who will choose expensive items.

One such festival in Bellevue, Washington, is said to be the oldest open-air festival of this sort on the West Coast—it has been held for twenty-eight years. It runs from Friday (with a noon opening hour) till sundown on Sunday. The festival is crowded the entire time, and it is not at all unusual for an artist or craftsman to earn $3,000 to $4,000.

The attendance at local festivals is closely tied to location. If the event is held in beautiful, spacious school grounds well off the beaten path, you may be certain that the public just is not going to make the effort to get there. The greater the distance from the main traffic arteries, the fewer the people who will attend. You may say that in such cases those who do make the effort to get there are likely to be more seriously interested than the general run of attendees at a central festival. Somehow, light attendance has an effect on the pocketbook . . . where relatively few people attend a festival, you often find that little money is being spent.

Sponsorship of the festival is the next important factor. In a community where the business people believe that the event contributes to their general well-being, you are certain of a royal welcome. Everything possible will be done to help you make a success of the show. It is even likely that the committee has made arrangements for a lounge area, with rest rooms. On Sunday that can become very important in some locations.

The festival sponsored by an art group probably ranks after that backed by the business community. Here you will find the committee far more conscious of who you are—this rarely occurs at the affairs sponsored by the businessmen. If you are completely unknown, it is quite likely that some of those who have volunteered to help run the festival will make it plain that you are lucky to have a chance to take part. But in spite of the fact that the art-oriented group tends to be very impressed with one's reputation as an artist—or lack thereof—such affairs are almost always reasonably well run and successful.

A totally different category of festivals is springing up: those sponsored by a group that uses the festival as a way to raise money. In a few cases, it is a purely commercial venture. In others, it is strictly a way to raise money for some worthy cause (see Chapter 9). Perhaps the most important detail about such festivals is that no matter how well advertised, no matter how worthy the cause, the buying public has the idea that once they have paid to get into the festival they are there for entertainment and not for buying.

Now that we have covered some of the important points to think about when you are invited to participate at some event, we will turn to more detailed consideration of just what you can do to make a success of the affair.

Gather as much background information as possible. Talk to anyone you know who has taken part in the festival; add to your list as you go along; try to find out what to expect. You may discover that a festival has no clear pattern—it may vary considerably from one year to the next. Whatever information you gather can be put to good use in getting yourself ready for the show. Do not hesitate to call anyone whose name comes up as having been part of such a festival. Almost without exception, craftsmen are glad to help a newcomer with information about their experiences.

When you have as much information as possible about what to expect during the festival, you now begin to plan your booth. Again, the situation varies greatly. In some cases, there are strict requirements; each booth must fit into a pattern. Many festivals, however, do not have rules about the way you display your wares.

Really, there are three primary considerations about the area from which you expect to sell.

1. **You want the potential buyers to see what you have.** This means that the display must be organized with careful consideration to making the best possible impression. Important items should be given space. You can crowd the low-cost items but keep the area with expensive pieces uncluttered. Consider eye level and the distance from which the attendees will view your work. Do everything possible to display your pieces attractively—make the booth one at which *you* would stop to browse.

2. The problem of security cannot be ignored. Costly items must be placed so that they are not easily stolen. It may be necessary to have glass cases for certain items for safekeeping. You can be sure of one thing: there will be numerous attempts to shoplift from your booth. If you go too far and make it impossible for people to pick things up and look at them, it is likely that sales will be slim. But unless you do everything possible to protect your merchandise, you will lose a great deal during any festival.

No easy solution exists for shoplifting. Many experienced craftsmen adopt the general practice of having low-cost items easily available for handling—as well as for shoplifting. Place one or two baskets of "the bottom of the barrel" near the edge of the table and allow handling of such items without question. Most people *do* want to pick things up and look at them, so let them handle pieces you might normally discard rather than your best items. Just realize ahead of time that you will have pieces stolen and do everything possible to keep theft to a minimum.

3. The matter of getting set up for the festival and dismantled afterwards should also be considered well ahead of time. You can spend more time constructing and removing the booth than you do talking with customers. Of course, the nature of your handcrafts plays an important part here—a jeweler has less of a problem than a potter. Do everything possible in the way of good planning to make this task quick and simple.

Essentially the same situation arises with each festival that you attend, so streamlining the operation will save you fatigue as well as time.

The three considerations are vital: an attractive display; reasonable security for your merchandise; and the ease with which the booth is established and removed. However, there are still other points to keep in mind, all of less importance but fairly essential.

Keep personal comfort in mind when planning your booth and display. A chair that wasn't really comfortable to begin with gets mighty wearing after a long day. Always anticipate heat or rain. Be prepared for weather changes. You can be badly blistered from sitting in the sun for prolonged periods . . . and you can be mighty uncomfortable when it's raining just enough to keep you wet but not hard enough to close down the show.

In conclusion, remember to take adequate change—always more than you really need—as well as your cards and other printed matter.

Perhaps you are now wondering why nothing has been said about what fees festivals charge, or what kind of sales commission is expected? If you have done your homework properly, as detailed in the preceding chapters, you are not really concerned much about these things. Your price structure will accommodate any normal fee and/or commission without problem. If you have not worked through the pricing formula for your handcrafts, then the art festival may be highly unprofitable for you, no matter how much you sell.

Regardless of the nature of the festival, there is always one way in which you can improve your sales picture: demonstrate! By giving the audience the opportunity to watch an artist in action, you are creating additional interest—and bringing in more sales. If the nature of your handcraft is such that some noise is also made . . . that's all the better. I have found that a demonstration of what seems the simplest technique used in jewelry work can tip the difference between borderline success and boom.

Try to plan an activity that takes little time yet produces real results. If it takes all day to complete an item, no one is going to stay to watch. If you can produce finished work quickly, many people will want to watch you through more than one cycle.

The jewelry craftsman can always find something that goes quickly and makes some noise —thus attracting attention. A simple hammered and stamped band ring with an unsoldered joint (adjustable!) certainly fills the bill. They are going to be a bit rough, under the circumstances, so you can well afford to offer them at bargain prices. With this approach you may have a line standing in front of you all day waiting for you to do a one-of-a-kind band ring while the prospective customer watches. If you have never done this sort of thing, the greatest surprise will be the kinds of people who will stand and wait for you to make an item for them. You know that what you are doing is simple and that the finished items are rough, but the buying public does like to see the artist in action.

Along with the many types of festivals, more and more opportunities arise for the craftsman to display and sell at local, state, or regional fairs. Originally, the main attraction at such a fair was the circus. The midway and the circus brought in the paying customers, who had little time or interest for the exhibits: the prize livestock, beautiful canned vegetables, etc. The midway is still part of most fairs, even though the circus has almost vanished. Possibly, with less entertainment today, there is more interest in the exhibits. I doubt it. The exhibiting craftsman who sells his work at a fair can expect it to be a bit rougher going than at the local art festival. At the latter, most of the people would at least claim to have some interest in seeing the art. But at a fair it is strictly entertainment. It is unlikely that those attending a fair are going to buy anything except your least expensive items. The sale of expensive work is very rare in such surroundings. So if you want to try this as a possible way to sell your handcrafts, be prepared to entertain the customers and to sell low cost items.

The fair is usually a yearly affair that lasts only a few days. The closest equivalent to this is the flea market that is open for long periods, perhaps all year. If you have not visited such an area, by all means do so. The flea market is crowded with a great variety of merchandise at every conceivable price level. Some of it is plain junk hardly worth taking home with you. But many items are likely to be costly indeed. The flea market often attracts good numbers of people and becomes one more form of public entertainment. There is every indication that lots of buying is done at the flea markets, but it does not look as though the merchants are getting rich quickly. If you want to try the flea market, by all means go ahead. However, I think it is possible that while you may sell well, it is even more likely that you will spend more time being a salesman than being a craftsman.

6

Consignment Selling

In the original draft of the manuscript for this book, this chapter was entitled, How to Get Off to a Bad Start—Consignment.

My negative view of consignment has been changed somewhat because it has been demonstrated to me that consignment sales can work and work well. However, the unique problems associated with consignment make it imperative that the beginning handcrafter understands how to handle it.

Consignment sales have been an accepted practice in the fine arts field for a very long time. Undoubtedly, this will continue to be true. Few shops are willing to buy the work of an unknown artist on the assumption that it will sell at a fair price. Of course, we are talking about original art now, not reproductions. Art reproductions are bought routinely by retail stores. The big difference is in the low selling price. The shop owner cannot afford to speculate on costly items.

For the individual who wants to begin selling his handcrafts, consignment is frequently nothing but bad news. Usually, the problems are directly related to the distance between the craftsman's location and the retail shop. However, even under the most favorable circumstances, consignment creates unique problems.

Generally speaking, the craftsperson who leaves items on consignment does so simply because he has found no other way to expose his work for sale. The shop accepts the handcrafts for one of two reasons: they cannot afford to buy the items for resale, or—and not to be overlooked—items are accepted on consignment that would not be bought even if the till was full. For example, the candle craftsman believes that the local beauty parlor might be able to sell his work. When approached, the shop owner will not be enthusiastic; candles are far removed from his normal business. He might well be persuaded to try these items on consignment, but the odds are that he would not buy them outright at any price.

The specialty craft shop that works only on consignment is not a parallel to the beauty parlor that was uncertain about taking the candles. The craft shop that accepts on consignment but will not buy is possibly unwilling to speculate on the work of unknown craftsmen. It is common practice for such a store to buy from some craftsmen while working on consignment with others.

At the beginning of this chapter, we mentioned the first potential difficulty relating to consignment: the physical distance between the handcrafter and the retail outlet. Happily, some shops operate by mail; they provide hobbyists with a highly efficient consignment service. But in all too many cases, the shop that is physically distant is likely to pose problems. The handcrafter will finally assume that slow payment and little information on sales progress is inevitable when working on consignment.

In passing note, art galleries are probably the worst possible consignment situation for the individual. The galleries that accept consignment crafts generally do little with them. It seems generally accepted that a display of crafts rounds out the work shown in the art gallery. Consequently, since most of the galleries' clientele concentrates on the artwork, there is often little buying action in the craft section.

Frequently, the shop most willing to accept consignment handcrafts is one that just does not have the money to operate on a buy-and-sell basis. Thus no matter how pure the intent of the shop owner, he will experience a constant temptation to operate on the craftsperson's money. The handcrafter brings in his work and it is immediately put on display. Within a few days, a number of items have been sold but the craftsman's check is not due until the end of the month. At that time, current bills are pressing. After these are paid, there may be no money in the till for the handcrafter. This action is not planned or intentional, but the shop owner operates with minimum cash resources. When bills are due, inevitably the craftsman will not be paid until next month.

Even if problems of regular payment do not arise, other major difficulties are traditionally associated with consignment. Here is the way it often works in practice: The beginning hobbyist hears of a shop accepting items on consignment but it is some distance from him. He makes the effort to visit the shop—spending a half or full day in the process—and leaves a number of items on consignment. Both the hobbyist and the operator of the shop clearly understand that accounting and payment is to be made at the end of each month. At the end of the first month, some items have been sold . . . the craftsman gets his check right on time and is delighted that he has found a good outlet for his items.

Two or three months may go by in the same way, the handcrafter more and more delighted with what he has discovered. Then comes a month when there is no check and no report. Knowing that the staff is busy, the handcrafter is reluctant to bother them. This is the first sensitive area. A visit to the shop will cost considerable time and effort. A telephone inquiry may arouse hostility. The store owner does not appreciate being checked on in such manner. A mail inquiry is likely to get a slow response.

At this point, the relationship between the craftsperson and the shop is strained. The former resents what has happened; possibly, his resentment will show through no matter what form his inquiry may take. Evidently, the craftsman's resentment is going to cause a similar response from the store owner.

If we assume that the store operator is making a genuine effort to do the right thing, here is probably what has happened: consignment items that have been passed over by the customers for three months or so just are not likely to sell, unless the shop has constantly changing customers. In a relatively static situation, most of the potential buyers have been exposed to the unsold items within two or three months. Merchandise that is not moving well is rarely displayed in the front window. It is relegated to a corner and finally a back room where it all gathers dust. By now, the shop owner has reached the point where he wishes the handcrafter would pick up his junk. Since he has not kept up his records and reports well, he is reluctant to raise the issue.

While this is happening in the store, the hobbyist is experiencing further deterioration in his relationship with the shop. He may go by and see that his work is poorly displayed, perhaps dusty. But he does not quite know what to do about it. After all, his work did sell well in the beginning. Maybe things will pick up again soon. Eventually, there comes a time when the hobbyist is unwilling to face up to the reality of what has happened. He may leave his work permanently unsold with the shop.

If you are willing to get your feet wet and try consignment selling, do so with full awareness of the potential problems and with the determination to avoid them.

It is probably essential, on making the first contact, that you let it be known that you are aware of the potential hazards of consignment selling. Explain to the store owner that you realize some items just will not move and that knowing this you will return at a stated time and *exchange* fresh work for that which is unsold. You are likely to make a firm friend. You have made it clear that you will help him by setting up a system to move unsold items from the shop automatically.

This point cannot be overemphasized. A system must be agreed upon in the very beginning. While some shop owners may have their own system to handle the matter, the probability is that you—the craftsperson—will have to take the initiative.

In actual practice, after discussion with a store, the jewelry craftsman leaves his work, saying, "I'll see you at the end of the month and I'll replace items that have sold. If by that time you have decided that any item isn't likely to sell for whatever reason, then I'll replace that too. There's no way to outguess the buying public. Something that won't sell here might be the first thing to go in another location."

What has been accomplished by setting up this system? First, you make it known to the shop owner that you are aware of his problems and intend to work with him to keep them to a minimum. Equally important, you have set up a routine in which you will call at the end of each month. Naturally, you will then expect your check for items that have sold. You are making the call to help the proprietor. At the same time, you are ensuring that regular monthly accounting takes place.

Consignment on this basis can and does work. However, something else has happened in the process. When making such calls, you are wearing the hat of the businessman rather than that of the handcrafter. Time spent in transacting such business is lost permanently in respect to producing handcrafts. Were the consignment items priced to take this into consideration (see Chapter 2)? If not, there is a net loss here that cannot be avoided.

Perhaps on reading this you will conclude that you do not want to spend your time running around checking on the consignment outlet, etc. You do not wish to be a businessman—you want to be a producing craftsman. At that point, the thing to do is to face up to it. If you cannot find someone to do this for you, and if you are unwilling to do it, you had best forget the idea of putting your handcrafts out on consignment.

If you are inclined to be cautious about financial matters or if your handcrafts are costly, there is one more fact to be considered: the legal implications of consignment. While verbal agreements are likely to be adequate, it seems prudent to put things into writing. Work up a brief written description of how *you* plan to operate. When you give it to the shop owner say, "You can see I believe in putting things in writing. That way no one can ever be misunderstood." The owner will almost certainly agree with you, so you continue, "Now you have my proposal in writing, and I'd like to ask you to sign for the items I leave with you."

If the person has just agreed that it is a good

idea to have things in writing, it is rather difficult for him to do anything but sign for items left on consignment. Should the shop owner decline to follow this procedure, you conclude that you were wise to ask . . . and take your handcrafts where someone will accept the responsibility for them.

Now, what about the financial arrangement between you and the shop having your products on consignment? What can be expected in the way of payment, percentage, etc.? The normal arrangement is that consignees are paid at the end of the month. By the time that bookkeeping has been done, this really means about the first week of the next month. In some cases, shops report and pay only on sixty day intervals. But this must be clearly understood from the very beginning.

How much does the shop get? It seems that a minimum for consignment goods is 25 percent. More frequently it is 33⅓ percent. This figure is, of course, based on *your* established retail price for the things you produce.

No doubt you will react strongly to the idea that the shop takes a third of the retail price when, really, they did nothing but display the merchandise and collect the money for sales. If this bothers your frugal streak, an alternate method can be considered: a consignment salesman, who handles the work for you. However, while the use of such a salesperson means you can remain at your workbench, the normal commission is one third. If the retail outlet and the salesperson handling your merchandise each are paid a third, obviously you—the producer—are left with a third. One's first reaction to this arrangement is that it is totally unacceptable. But suppose you produce enough to sell wholesale (see Chapter 8)? The wholesaler's commission for craft items is rarely less than 50 percent, sometimes more. We will work with that average figure for our illustration.

Once you have established a retail price for

your crafts, you decide to sell them wholesale. If you take the time and effort to establish the contacts, travel to and from the buyers' offices, as well as spend time on the different appointments and interviews displaying your crafts and discussing business, then you have earned a commission—certainly all that time has not been spent creating more merchandise. If, however, it is not practical for you to handle such wholesale work as outlined above, you must find someone who can.

Usually, the wholesale commission is in the range of 20 percent of gross sales. If we assume a retail price of $1, the commissions to be deducted are:

Wholesale	50¢	(50 percent of retail)
Sales commission	10¢	(20 percent of gross
Total	60¢	—wholesale)

The craftsman-manufacturer is, therefore, left with 40 cents of each retail dollar.

Since, when the same item is sold by a consignment outlet, the store and the salesperson each take a third of the retail dollar, you are left with 33⅓¢. There you have the two figures: 40¢ on the dollar from selling wholesale, 33⅓¢ on the dollar from selling on consignment.

The difference is not too great if we assume that your production volume is still limited. Our personal choice is to sell by the wholesale method in preference to the consignment route. We recommend consignment as a last resort . . . when all else fails. If you do go that route, keep in mind that you will end up with only a third of the retail dollar. Here we come full circle and reiterate the vital importance of establishing an initial price that covers all expenses adequately while also allowing for a profit.

A relatively new type of consignment selling may be available in your area. However, to utilize it, one has to produce a rather significant quantity. It is not likely that you will use this selling method until you employ several people.

This form of volume consignment selling has to do with the specialty salesman, who puts his wares out on consignment. In this case, the salesman himself buys the product, then he consigns them and collects from the retailer. Here, the craftsperson sells to the consignment salesman rather than to the shop. This means that the craftsperson does not have to pay a commission to the salesman.

It immediately seems to promise only good, doesn't it? Thus you collect for what you sell when you deliver! Thus you have no investment sitting in retail outlets. The salesman pays you, then places the items on retail consignment. What is the drawback, you ask? Well, for this type of operation, the specialty salesman just cannot pay more than 20 percent of the established retail price. You, the designer and the manufacturer, retain 20 percent of the retail dollar. Perhaps it just does not seem fair?

Relax, no one will force you to sell to the specialty salesman at 20 percent of retail. Nor is it essential that you put your items out on consignment for 33⅓ percent of the retail dollar. You have absolute freedom to select any sales method or refuse it.

Your alternate approach is to handle the sales yourself. This means that instead of spending time at your workbench, you will be cooling your heels waiting to see the buyer. You may very well end up selling your products for as much if not more than any salesman. However, think of the cost in your time and effort. Was the result really worth this?

By now you should have the idea. The sensible approach, indeed the only approach if you are to become self-supporting, is to price your products so that their sale—by whatever method—is at a price that gives you a fair return for time, effort and materials. If your original prices were established without consideration of the marketing problem, withdraw these items and start all over again. If the items you produce do not bring a fair return, you will never become self-supporting.

7

Your Own Retail Gallery

The title for this chapter makes it clear that the decision has already been made. You are going to establish a retail shop. You know that it will not be easy, that it will create lots of new problems, but you have decided that this is the way to go!

The retail shop always seems a better method than selling on consignment or wholesale or even from your own home studio. Somehow the idea of having your own small shop and getting full retail price for everything you produce comes across to all of us as being ideal.

The retail outlet certainly offers the best way to display your handcrafts to their best. All other display techniques are makeshift at best. And while the fairs, carnivals, and festivals do attract lots of interest, logically, a retail shop would establish a better relationship with those who buy the things you make.

I feel that once you have arrived at the major decision to open your own store, the next step is the name. This should come right now, before you go out and check locations. That name can be all important. You want something that catches attention, is easily remembered, and gives just the right impression. Here is a suggestion—make it a gallery.

"But," you protest, "I'm not really an artist and it really won't be a gallery." I'm not sure that that is the right attitude. You will remember that this was discussed in the first chapter—how important it is for the craftsman to understand that while one may not be producing work in the fine arts category, handcrafting is an art and, under one of the many definitions of the word, the craftsman or hobbyist can be considered an artist. Even if your ego is humble!

I have very good reasons for suggesting the name of *gallery* for the small handcraft retail outlet. In Chapter 4 I proposed that your home operation be defined as *studio* because of the many advantages gained by the use of that word. Again, for the retail shop, the use of *gallery* in the name can be a real asset.

A gallery will get all kinds of publicity (at no cost) that the shop just does not get. And when you open a retail shop, publicity is the thing that can make you. Lack of it can break you. To make it even more beautiful, the type of publicity a gallery will be given generally cannot be bought.

The next thing is to choose a location; this is always a compromise. The right locations are always too costly in the beginning. In Seattle there is a new development, Pioneer Square. The present center of the area is known as the Grand Central Building. Most of the foot traffic in the area goes by the door of the Grand Central Building. It has recently been redecorated, and an outstanding job was done. Today, rents in the Pioneer Square area are directly related to distance from the Grand Central Building. No doubt the best spot for a gallery would be the closest vacant shop to the Grand Central Building. But go one or two blocks away in either direction and rents may easily be half what they would be at the more desirable location.

So as you reluctantly decide that the choice locations are not possible at the moment, what other factors should you take into consideration? Well, if you were thinking about opening a used car lot, it is a well-known fact that your best location would be somewhere along "used car row." Every urban area has such an area . . . usually rather well defined. Of course, all the competition is there, but then that's also where people go when they think of buying a used car.

For your gallery location make a firm decision to find a spot that is part of a colony of specialty shops in the arts, crafts, and related fields. The true art gallery (there are still a few!), the antique shop, the specialty food shop, the leather shop and all other such shops. You *may* be able to draw traffic to an isolated location, but it is far easier to go where a pattern exists.

Perhaps the next important consideration is the proximity of public parking and public transportation. You can be on a very busy street where traffic flows at all hours, but if there is no convenient parking you will get only the walking traffic. Over a period of two or three years, I found it very enlightening to watch a small corner shop at a busy intersection considerably out of the retail shop area. Almost every type of craft you can imagine has been in that location. The average life of a tenant is four to six months. Because of the heavy load of automobile traffic, one might think it is a good location. But there is no parking of any kind for several blocks. What little walking traffic there is seems to be just passing through the area on the way to somewhere else.

Once you have picked a location and rented or leased for a specific term you are ready to get the sales area prepared. Here you can easily demolish your budget for a long time to come. The cost of doing a shop front the way you would like to would probably ruin you. You need not necessarily have expensive decor to appeal to potential customers. It is well accepted today that specialty shops, such as you are planning, operate on a minimum of cash reserve. The public does not mind low-cost decorations *so long as they are attractive.*

With the present interest in anything old, you can find low-cost decorations. Anything that was commonplace before the birth of people who are under forty years is old *if it has passed out of use!* You don't have to be ancient to remember the horse and buggy days. Who, forty to fifty years ago, would have believed that any relic of a horse-drawn vehicle could command attention in the center of a smart department store?

If possible, something old that pertains to your craft is always good. It seems that before long a manual typewriter will be a collector's item. A cash register that can ring up a maximum sale of $5 will always attract attention. The specialty coffee shop today that has a hand-operated coffee grinder wouldn't trade that "antique" for anything.

The important point is simply this: keep your initial costs to an absolute minimum. The fact that you are new in your location will attract a certain amount of traffic. Other business will come to you through the grapevine. If you have had students, by all means make certain that they know you are opening a gallery.

You may wish to have a "grand opening." By all means do so if you have a mailing list large enough to warrant this. How big a list is large enough? That depends on many things. If you start on a minimum budget, as we have assumed in this chapter, a mailing to fifty potentially interested people is large enough to justify an opening event.

In the long run, your mailing list is possibly the best way to advertise for a while. Whenever there is a special display or a special occasion, let your mailing list do the job.

Although this step is dependent upon the nature of the handcrafts you produce, my next advice is to arrange your retail shop so that you can work constructively during the time when no customers are in the shop. It is important that you do not lose time that could be devoted to production of new items. While you may not be able to do everything in the environment of your retail shop, possibly you can do something.

Here again, the advice to begin operating on a minimum budget pays off. If you have low-cost decorations and display areas, those who come in to look around won't be bothered in the least by seeing your workbench in the same area. As a matter of fact, I consider a visible location of your workbench and the tools of your craft as a real asset to the shop. Remember that today people appreciate handmade items to a far greater degree than was apparent a few years ago.

If more than one craftsman is involved in the retail shop, you should seriously consider having someone actively producing as much of the time as possible. Of course, people who drop in are likely to waste production time when they want to see what's going on and be told about it. In the long run, it is generally time well spent.

When the time comes that the gallery has prospered to the extent that you are able to hire a clerk, you have another important decision to make. Your target is to have this employee handle clerical work in order to free you for craft production. With this in mind, the type of person hired needs careful consideration.

Obviously, the person who represents you in the retail shop should have a pleasing, outgoing personality, integrity, etc. If this person is either a practicing handcrafter or is seriously interested in learning something of your craft, his presence will be a double asset.

Unless you go into mass production, your gallery will always be a handcraft store. The people who shop there will always be interested in the handcraft aspect of the operation. Thus the retail salesperson should be personally involved in the handcrafts in one way or another.

Remember now, that we are not talking about a shop that draws transient tourists. The place in the lobby of a hotel, for example, may carry an assortment of fine craft items and sell them in some quantity. But such a store depends almost entirely upon the tourist and needs a quite different salesperson. The majority of the purchases are bought as gifts—and here the good salesperson can do a very effective job even though knowing little about the merchandise. So, do try to employ someone who is actually involved in a craft.

Undoubtedly, a varied display of craft items from allied fields will increase the interest in your gallery. People who browse for ceramics, leather, candles, glass and other handcrafts are quite likely to be interested in buying your products as well. Thus nothing but good can come from having an assortment of handcrafts displayed.

However, today one cannot ignore security. Small items of value simply must be kept under glass in locked cases. Thefts can quickly put you into a loss rather than a profit situation. Where possible, keep the costly items close together; it is much easier to give them adequate care that way. The problem of shoplifting is so severe that large department stores have plainclothes security agents always circulating.

It is an established fact that more small stores fail in the first year than survive. This is because few people realize that it is virtually unknown for a new enterprise to show a profit before at least a year. You can expect it to take six to twelve months for the gallery to draw enough traffic to pay its own way. Should you break even—if profits cover expenses—at the end of only three months, you will be exceptionally fortunate. Thus the decision to open a gallery should not be made until you have sufficient reserve funds to operate for at least a year. The idea that you will operate the shop yourself and stay in a low-rent area is really not getting around the fact that you will operate at a loss for some time. While you may avoid some of the obvious dollar outflow by such compromises, you will have hidden costs not easily evaluated. It may be that a difference of $25 a month in rent can mean success or failure. The choice of the lower rent area is not necessarily good business. If you do not get the traffic at that location, you will not be able to pay the rent for long, no matter how low it is.

Your retail gallery must pay its own way. You must have a system for properly identifying costs so that this operation does not get a free ride from the other part of your work—that of producing handcrafts. A system for accounting so that the gallery is what is called a separate cost center is necessary. Unless this is done, you can go for months without being certain whether or not the shop is operating at a profit or at a loss.

Thus proper accounting requires that you "sell" your work to the gallery at wholesale prices. In this manner, you will know if you are producing your handcrafts profitably or not. At the same time, the gallery must account for all items received. Thus each phase of the operation stands apart, for accounting purposes.

In the end analysis, if you want to open a retail shop you must price your handcrafts at the wholesale level. Perhaps this concept should have been introduced somewhat earlier, but it might easily have caused you to become negative about your own retail outlet.

The thesis of this book is that the producing craftsman must understand what it means to produce his work at prices comparable to those of a regular wholesale structure. Until he can do so there is no way to avoid major problems. Sooner or later you will have to learn how to price and produce at wholesale prices. The failure to understand the implications of this and to work out the resulting price structures and accounting systems can only cause you grief in the long run. Certainly, it will be impossible for you to become self-supporting through the sale of your handcrafts.

Thus the retail shop has its drawbacks. Perhaps they are greater than you realized. It may well be that after you see all of the problems involved you will decide that for you there must be a better way. But regardless of your decision, let it be made in full understanding of what is involved.

In summary, this chapter details some of the problems associated with a retail outlet of your own. It may very well be that this does not look as attractive a venture to you now as it first did, before the various potential hazards were outlined. The major problems associated with getting the gallery started and keeping it going until it can pay its own way can easily divert you from your main interest: production of your own handcrafts.

Every activity that uses energy drains just that much from both your time and your creative effort. This possibility simply must not be ignored. Once again, it is essential that you analyze your approach to the handling of a retail outlet.

If you decide that a retail store is just not for you—and if this decision reflects a change of heart—that is not a sign of weakness. On the contrary, it is a sign of strength. Recognize that you *can* change your mind.

Perhaps there is one main point to keep in mind when you are reviewing the question of whether or not to open a retail outlet to sell your crafts: such an outlet is not an automatic solution to the problem of how to sell your items. The chances are that your life will become even more complicated through undertaking such a venture.

Go slowly. Make certain that your decisions are based on a firm analysis of all the factors involved. When you do send out those announcements for your opening . . . lots of luck!

Wholesale Selling

If you are like so very many craftsmen who want to do only one-of-a-kind work, no production runs, you may feel that this chapter has nothing for you. Not so fast! The fact that your handcrafts may be sold wholesale certainly does not mean that you are getting into routine production effort. What does wholesale mean really? It means that you are selling your work to someone who in turn expects to sell it at retail, for a profit.

Since you were willing to put your work out on consignment, what is the difference? The items on consignment were sold, weren't they? But you did not sell them, did you?

You are more than likely ready to reply, "The difference is this. On consignment I get two-thirds of the retail value and the shop receives only one-third. If I sold wholesale I would only receive half the retail price. That does not seem quite right to me."

This basic analysis is right. The wholesaler expects to buy at no more than half the retail price, frequently less. But there is one other thing to consider: when you sell wholesale, you are paid immediately. You do not have to wait and see whether it will sell. You do not have the items sitting in a shop for several months while you wonder if they will ever sell.

We went over the mechanics of establishing a price formula in Chapter 2. The structure definitely took into consideration selling wholesale. So if your prices accurately reflect all costs and profit, you can sell wholesale and *as a handcrafter* make just as much as if you sold the items retail yourself."

Someone will challenge this immediately. "How can I make as much selling as if I had sold retail?" However, that was not how the statement read. Go over it again. "If you have properly structured your prices, you can sell wholesale and *as a handcrafter* make just as much as if you had sold the items retail yourself."

When you personally do the retail selling, you just are not wearing your craftsman hat. At that point, you have become a retail merchant. In that role, as the retailer, you should make a profit. Separate the functions, for they are miles apart. If you want to do your own selling only to retail areas, not wholesale, do not mistakenly think that you as a craftsman have made all of that profit. Mr. Retailer must also be considered. If you omit him, he is literally donating time and effort.

Once again, the emphasis is upon the importance of recognizing your role. If you are willing to be only a craftsperson and will not spend time selling retail, no one has any quarrel with that. If this is your target, it is also clear that someone else must handle the selling for you. Perhaps the easiest way is to sell wholesale.

The wholesaler who buys handcrafts for resale is likely to be a local merchant who plans to sell the items retail. In this case, he expects the retail price to be at least double what he paid. Wholesale purchasers for, say, hardware and groceries do not expect as much markup as do merchants who deal in specialty goods such as handcrafts. After all, the risk involved in groceries and hardware is minimal, while the risk associated with handcrafts is high. Something that is the fashion today may be completely forgotten tomorrow. The purchaser of handcrafts does not expect to sell everything he buys at full retail.

All too frequently, craftsmen who do not wish to accept the role of wholesaler, price their work without including costs for the selling function. In effect, they are selling the items retail at wholesale prices. This is the fundamental error common to hobbyists who begin selling their work. Unless the cost of selling is taken into consideration, these items are underpriced.

However, it is important to consider the type of items that can be sold wholesale. Anything that the purchaser is willing to buy can be sold wholesale. If it is one-of-a-kind rather than from a production run, it is still a legitimate item for wholesaling. Since payment is immediate, this selling method has the advantage over consignment.

You may wish to sell as much as you can retail, then let your excess be sold through the wholesale method. That is a perfectly correct decision. You may have picked the best possible compromise. It is almost always possible for the craftsman to retail a certain amount of his crafts with little time and effort. However, after these simple contacts have been made and part of your production sold, you still have the rest of the package to consider. Unless you are careful, you may fall into the trap of spending too much time and effort handling the retail sales. Then your production will drop to the level that solves the problem of having excess to sell!

If, on the other hand, you become involved in production and wish to expand, it is almost certain that the wholesale approach will be preferable. This is especially true if you employ two or three people. At that point, you have become a small manufacturer. Possibly, your personal production of handcrafts will drop off somewhat.

In order to sell regularly on a wholesale basis, several points must be considered carefully. In retail selling, you are not likely to sell additional items to the same purchaser. Of course, you will have repeat customers, but even your best retail customers are not likely to buy from you more than once or twice a year.

When you sell wholesale, you are selling to the same purchaser over and over again. The retail purchaser has relatively little basis for comparison between his current purchase and anything you have previously produced. Each item is basically a closed situation complete in itself. Few people are likely to review your stock and comment, "From what I see here, it looks as though your quality has changed."

However, the very thing the wholesale purchaser looks for each time is consistency. He has bought from you before and returned because those items sold well. He knows that if he has the same quality again he can sell again. If your quality varies (whether up or down) he is in a different position. Someone has noted that if you want to sell wholesale, it would be better to have consistently poor merchandise than to be erratic . . . good work one time, poor the next.

Industry usually exercises quality control. Most products are marked, "Inspection." This indicates a consistent standard. Whatever the name, you can be certain that the production worker wishes it did not exist. Any worker is likely to be somewhat erratic: top quality work one day, a lower standard the next. If work is not checked at times, the quality will slip.

Here again, you the handcrafter are forced into yet another role: inspector for quality control. It is not easy. Make no mistake about it. This kind of effort will force severe self-discipline upon you.

How can an individual who enjoys producing original work become involved in a production effort? If his handcrafts are largely hobby and incidental to his total income, he can avoid this problem almost indefinitely. But if the time comes when he decides to go into the craft field of his choice to support himself completely from the income, he may be forced to face the economic realities as well as the enjoyment factors. For those who wish to use their craft field as a primary source of income, there is no choice.

Once again, personal illustration is in order. After a good many years spent in engineering administration at the Boeing Company, I considered resigning that field to go into handcrafted jewelry full time. It really wasn't too tough a decision because the previous year our handcrafts had brought in a most satisfactory financial total. But the regular paycheck is very reassuring, along with the paid vacation, paid sick leave, comprehensive medical insurance, etc. Once my wife and I had reached that decision and found that we could adjust to the uncertainties of an income that varied greatly from week to week, we had to resolve another important point. We could remain a "mamma-pappa" shop indefinitely, and no doubt do very well financially. But a time would come —and before too many years—when we could no longer function as producing craftsmen. What then? Even assuming we were able to accumulate income for retirement, the business would die at that point.

The transition into a function that would go on after we were no longer able to be successful producing craftsmen ourselves had to be accomplished—this demanded a different approach. We felt that wholesale selling was obviously one of the necessities.

Now no one who is accustomed to creating individual pieces only is likely to enjoy any form of production. In my own case, it isn't so much an active dislike for production work, just that it is not easy to enjoy it. In the end, production work provides its own challenge. One can find something meaningful in it . . . provided you look! In the process of trying to get production over as quickly as possible, it is only reasonable to try to find swifter and easier work methods. In the end, the discovery of better methods becomes a form of real satisfaction in itself. It offers a different type of creativity from that of handcrafting, but it is just as real. Of course, once you are satisfied that there is simply no way to do the job more quickly or more easily, then the satisfaction and creativity have gone . . . then it really does become "dog work." So long as there is a possibility that one may find better, simpler, and faster ways to do things, the challenge remains. Incidentally, in the process of devising new ways, you discover fresh techniques.

Most important of all, the short cuts and new skills discovered in the process of getting the production work over swiftly can now be applied to the field of your first choice: creation of original and unique handcrafts. At this point, your capability as a producing handcrafter will be much greater than it was before you were forced to "waste time" doing production work!

My final comment on wholesaling of handcrafts concerns package or display. Do everything possible to stay away from this! You know as well as I do that today the package, or way displayed, counts as much as the contents. Let someone else do this. The problems and headaches in packaging will take you into a whole new field—one that is full of pitfalls.

We have now covered how wholesaling can affect your approach and work habits. We must also consider how you place your merchandise with wholesalers.

Those who have never sold anything may be reluctant to think of calling on wholesale buyers. The idea of an "important buyer" may intimidate one. It is well to know something about wholesale buyers and how they operate. Whether the buyer is the owner of the small corner craft shop or a full-time buyer for a chain of department stores, the attitude is much the same. When an unknown calls (by telephone, of course) and asks to show his wares, the buyer has no choice in the matter. He is almost compelled to see you. He simply cannot afford to miss out on something good. The buyer can reach a very fast decision, perhaps negative, but he still has to look. You are all the better off that he can made a swift decision. What if it took him the whole morning, or if he had to think about it for several weeks?

If the buyer is favorably impressed, you need to be able to tell him how much you can produce and how long it takes you to deliver after an order is placed. Don't let your desire to sell cause you to give unrealistic answers. If you quote a delivery date that you cannot meet, you will lose that account anyhow, so why not be sensible in the beginning and make no impossible promises.

It is really easy to get in to see the buyer. When you do, don't try to show him everything you have ever done. Pick out a few, a very few, items. If he wants to see more he will say so.

If you wish to sell through a representative to wholesale buyers, this is also possible. In most cases, the salesman is on commission, approximately 25 percent of the wholesale price for such specialities as handcrafts. Here again, if you did your homework in Chapter 2, your price structure enables you to offer the salesman an acceptable commission without altering your prices.

You can, if you so desire, use yet another method of wholesaling. It is not necessary that a salesman represent you. While there are obvious advantages to having someone show up in person to present your line, this can also be handled effectively by mail.

The buyer for any organization with numerous branches or shops can and will consider your handcrafts if sent in by mail in a manner that conforms to his specific requirements. Your problem is first to determine just what best suits the buyer. Your first letter should enquire for the ground rules. You should conform to these as closely as possible. Thus a letter to the buyer of the XYZ Company concerning your handcrafted products might be as follows:

Buyer, Handcrafts XXXXXXXXXXX ************
XYZ Company, xxxxxxxxxxxxxxxx   date
xxxxxxxxxxxxxxxxxxxxxxxxxxxxx

Please send information concerning your buying schedule and requirements for sending samples. It seems that my handcrafted products might well fit into your line, but in order to present them to you properly it would help greatly to know just how you wish this done.

Cordially yours

....

Note the absence of salutation above, no "Dear Sir" or "Dear Madam". Today this just is not necessary in that first letter. The response will give what you need to know for future letters. This first letter is just to determine whether you should make the effort to get a sample case together for this possible sale.

When making preparations for sending samples—according to instructions received in response to your enquiry—be certain that your samples conform to the rules given. Possibly, the buyer makes it clear that samples will be returned only at your expense. (In such cases, I feel that it is wise to write this one off to begin with and *not* ask for return of samples.) Anything you do to make it more difficult for the buyer is obviously going to work against you sooner or later. Conform to *his* basic ground rules; do not expect him to make an exception for you.

Never lose sight of the fact that the buyer has a definite job to do. He or she must do everything possible to obtain the best items at the lowest price for the operation. Thus your line *will* be considered. It may take the buyer only a quick glance to determine that it does not fit into plans for the retail shops. Or he may take a second and a third look. If the decision is negative that does not mean that the door is shut to this buyer from now on. He will be just as ready to take a look at your next submission as he was the first. When the buyer indicates that your handcrafted products are not right for him, that decision is based on present circumstances and certainly does not mean that you should not try again, with different items.

The buyer for a large organization has quite a bit to do after he decides that your products would sell in his operation. He must know that you can deliver in both quantity and quality and on a predetermined schedule. If he places an order with you and counts on delivery at a specified time, it is essential that this delivery date be met. Failure to deliver on schedule will put that buyer on the spot with *his* management.

So here again it is important that you do not

promise anything you cannot deliver. If you simply do not see any way to produce the volume of items the buyer would like to have, face up to that *before* you accept the order rather than waiting until the last minute.

Perhaps the most important thing to be noted from this chapter is that you *will* get consideration for your handcrafted products from even the largest merchandising chains. This is not to say that your path will be clear and problem free. The American merchandising system has its shortcomings, but it is true that the smallest producer can request—and get—consideration almost anywhere.

9

Worthy Causes: Selling for Sweet Charity

In spite of the fact that this chapter seems to contain largely negative comments, you cannot afford to miss selling at the charity functions. How in the world can you sort them out and know which is going to be good and which will be depressing and at best an enormous waste of time? The clues are easy to spot . . . and amazingly accurate. Since the emphasis is on the negative, the clues warning you to stand clear are also negative. Just keep your eyes open and you simply can't fail to spot these definitive pointers. If any one of the following clues is spotted, you are warned that the affair is likely to be bad. Make it a rule that if two or more negative clues are spotted, nobody can talk you into it regardless of how persuasive they may be!

First comes the small society or group that has an annual art sale. This is much like a small public art festival—except for the fact that a good portion of those who attend will expect to buy something as their contribution to the worthy cause.

The organization will get a fairly healthy cut out of anything that is taken in during such a function . . . on the other hand, they are very cooperative. Limited facilities are the rule rather than the exception, but the people who help make the function work are always pleasant and willing to do anything possible to assist you. Have you the message loud and clear? Take part in every such function possible. You can do nothing but good by being there, selling a certain amount and giving out your cards to all who admire your handcrafts.

You are not likely to make any large sales nor set a record for gross sales, but it will cost you time only and there are far too many plus factors about it to ignore this function. Please remember that exceptions to the general rule abound! This chapter outlines rather typical situations which are, of course, based primarily on personal experience.

The major negative clue to be on the watch for is publicity—or lack of! The worthy cause art festival that's likely to be right for you will not have a great amount of publicity. You *won't* hear it announced on television spots night and day; you *won't* see advertisements for it plastered on the sides of every transit bus in town; you *won't* find it all over the Sunday newspaper the week before the big event. The preferred kind of function for you to attend is the effort of a relatively small organization. They do not have the muscle to obtain massive publicity.

As a general rule, the greater the publicity, the more likely it is to be a flop for you, the producing craftsman. No matter how great the function might be for the sponsoring organization, if it leaves you wishing you had never heard of it, there is no way you can call it a success. So keep a weather eye out for publicity. If the person who invites you to take part leads off with a short dissertation on the grand publicity, that's your first warning . . . loud and clear.

Another detail usually bandied about regarding this well-publicized event is the enormous crowds drawn to it. Well, volume attendance does not mean volume craft sales. It *might* mean record sales of hot dogs and soft drinks and items that do not require careful consideration by the purchaser, such as toys for the children, home-baked goods, or plants. In addition, when such an affair has a history of large attendance, the organizers frequently request booth fees—I've known them to go as high as several hundred dollars.

Such an offer might sound enticing, especially since it is often coupled with the disarming remark, "no percentage of sales is taken by our committee." It can all sound very straightforward. Indeed, to clear your path the organizers will have booths set up and decorated . . . you won't even have to bring in a table or chair of your own. "Just let us know how many chairs you will need during the festival." The clincher will be the comment, "After all, you *know* your crafts sell so well at public functions."

Now back off a minute and see what this charity is asking of you. It is really very simple. They are letting you take all the risk. You pay a substantial fee well in advance of the festival and then if it is a bust that's your tough luck. The committee has fortunately collected from you in advance!

By now the pattern should be obvious. You rarely find clue one without clue two! Since you have been warned that the existence of two negative clues is all you need to stay clear of any such function, there is hardly any need for you to investigate this situation further. Decline pleasantly and firmly. Make it quite clear that you cannot be persuaded to change your mind!

If by any chance you are patsy enough to tell the committee that you'll think it over, search carefully for clue number three. The "happy experience" function that raises funds for their work by an annual fair or festival *will not charge admission.*

In direct contrast, the event that is likely to be pleasant for you will not ask for a registration fee, booth fee, or what have you. A simple arrangement that a certain percentage of everything you sell goes to the worthy cause is the *modus operandi.* This is highly practical—the organization is as willing as you are to take their chances. They are not looking for a sure thing.

If we examine in depth the reason our three negative clues are certain indications of trouble, you will note that the different viewpoints mean different methods. The well-organized, well-publicized festival insists on a donation at the gate. This screens out casual observers. It also makes possible all the wonderful publicity, the decorator-inspired decor, the marvelous facility, and the forty piece string band that plays continuously during most of the festival. If you hadn't been warned, you just might fall for that line of malarkey. Everything that has been said about the two previous negative clues goes double for number three. Admission or donations at the door mean only bad news for the craftsmen participating at the festival.

Take a look at you as a private individual attending such a function. You'll pat yourself on the back when you pay your donation. You've done your bit for charity. Off you go to be entertained and listen to that band. But are you likely to buy anything more than a bag of popcorn and a bottle of beer? Thousands of other spectators will also be wandering around watching the performing craftsmen, "They are really putting on quite a show, aren't they, Mother?"

To date, the writer knows of no exception to

negative clue number three. Remember, we are talking about worthy causes now. A few art festivals charge admission and are apparently successful, but they are not presented as charities. They are commercial enterprises, and there is no way those who attend can feel they have done their bit for charity when they present the ticket stubs at the door.

A final negative factor does exist. Clue number four: if the big event for the art festival is the auction, presided over by a well-known professional auctioneer (who is probably being paid a handsome fee), be advised that you'll undoubtedly find this auction one of your worst experiences.

No humiliation is as bad as public humiliation. When you see an apathetic audience prodded by an expert auctioneer for even a bid on many items, when you see fine handcrafts and art selling for ten cents on the dollar value, you could sit down and cry. Especially when it's *your* work that goes that way.

Usually, the auctioneer will find several categories for which he can generate not only interest but genuine enthusiasm. Some unexceptional pieces of handcrafted jewelry donated for a worthy cause have been auctioned at double their value. But frequently during that same auction, other fine handcrafts are virtually given away. You may be the fortunate one who can see some audience enthusiasm when your work is on the block. For every one such as you, ten others who worked just as hard as you did see their handcrafts labeled third or fourth-class by the bored and sophisticated audience.

You are likely to get not one but many such requests, for there has been a sharp growth of this type of activity in recent years. Sort them out carefully before making a decision. One can have a pleasant time and sell lots of handcrafts at smaller unadvertised affairs. But the chances are very good indeed that large, well-promoted, and highly advertised "fairs" will cause you nothing but grief.

One other related activity should be mentioned in this chapter. Numerous charities request donations—some of your own handcrafts—which they then sell to raise money. Again, this is becoming very common. At the sale, the participants may purchase at listed prices; in other cases, the items are sold by an experienced auctioneer. No one can guess what might happen at such an event. Your work may sell at high prices or virtually be given away. Try to be objective about this type of fundraising. A few questions might well be asked.

"Why are requests for donations made only to artists and craftsmen?" "Why not ask for donations from the grocery store, the hardware shop, and the service station?"

The whole purpose of the effort is to raise funds for a cause that everyone recognizes as worthy in every sense of the word. But the artist and the craftsman get such requests over and over. It hardly seems right that contributions of items for sale should come from a limited group.

Possibly, the items you donate will eventually bring additional business to you. Don't count on it. It's more likely that you will catch problems or complaints rather than more customers. If anything goes wrong with the donated item, be sure the purchaser will bring it back to you for action. One really has little choice in the matter—you either give in gracefully and try to do what is asked or flatly refuse. And you know as well as I that a flat refusal isn't going to do you any good. This repair work is another "donation" that can hardly be listed with the I.R.S.

By now you should have little doubt that the writer is quite negative on this subject. Not because of too many bad experiences. It took only a couple of such events for us to get a general impression of what to expect.

Perhaps my attitude may prove wrong. It may well be that the experiences described are limited to this geographic area. But I am ready to predict that the situation won't change with time or differ from one region to another.

10

Selling by Mail

Handcrafted work is sold by mail in considerable volume these days. There have always been a few individual craftsmen selling by mail order, but more and more the mails are used for sophisticated offerings.

For instance, you can send 25¢ and receive an 88-page color listing of handcrafts and Christmas cards. Now there's no way in the world that this catalog can be produced for that price, even when large numbers are printed. When you realize that the organization offering this brochure is none other than the Metropolitan Museum of Art, it really begins to sink in. Selling handcrafts by mail is big business today.

Various museums and art institutes offer color catalogs year after year. Obviously this practice pays off, otherwise it would be declining not growing. It is certain that a great deal of handcrafts will be sold by mail in the immediate future—perhaps yours.

Let us suppose that you have decided to try selling by mail. Various steps and decisions are necessary to get this program going.

Mail orders come in solely as the result of advertising. If we exclude radio and television spots, two prime methods are open: newspapers and magazines. These can be divided into two groups, publications with circulation, and those involved with direct mail.

First we will consider newspaper and magazine advertising. What type of publication will be best for you? Today there are so many, that you need to give close inspection to the most likely prospects. Make it a basic rule to advertise only in publications carrying lots of ads for selling by mail. Do not make the mistake of picking a magazine that has no such advertisements, thinking that you will thus get a jump on the market. If the magazine has been in existence for several years or more, you can be certain that it would have such ads if it were a good vehicle for mail-order selling. On the other hand, plenty of magazines are full of ads for mail order. You can be certain that some are having good results. You will remember the analogy we used previously about the used car lot. The best place to open such a place is on that strip of road where every other used car dealer is located. Go where the action is.

The magazine finally chosen should cover the best possible market for your handcrafts. If your work would appeal particularly to teenagers, choose a magazine in that field. If you are doing something that will be attractive mostly to housewives consider something like the general interest women's magazines.

Before you place that first ad, you must plan to run the same or similar advertisements in the same magazine for *at least* three consecutive issues, six would be better. The shotgun approach, placing one ad here, another there, etc., is not likely to give much result. It seems that the reading public gains confidence in a product when they see the same, or similar, ad appearing month after month. They are under the impression that people must buy that product or the ad would be discontinued. Generally they are right. Continuity in ads does more to inspire confidence than anything else you can do initially.

Go through the magazines that seem to be full of ads for mail orders, note which appeal to you and which you would normally hardly notice. What differences do you note in this survey? What common characteristics do the ads have that appeal to you personally?

As you define your thinking watch for one thing in the ads that catch your eye. How many items do they advertise? What sort of decision does the prospective customer have to make? In general, best results come from an ad that sharply limits the number of items offered. The purchaser's decision is a simple "Yes," or "No," rather than, "Would I like this one better than that one?".

Well-established businesses *do* offer choices, but for every one of these you can spot several other ads that offer only *one* item. The single item ad commands decision. The person who reads will buy or not buy. In either case, there has been a definite reaction and you have results from which to predict how future ads will do.

How much *profit* is likely to come in from your ads? You will be doing extremely well if, for a period of several months, you break even. If you generate enough business to pay for the ads, they are remarkably successful. The *real reason* for the ad (in most cases) is to develop a mailing list for possible repeat customers. You can't offer too many choices in a small ad. But you can offer unlimited choices in whatever literature you develop to send along with those first orders.

So, unless you have planned listings or some sort of catalogue to go with those mail orders, there really isn't too much point in placing the ad in the first place. While there will be times that ads for mail-order items do bring in a great deal of profitable business, this is the exception. Generally you will not make profit from a single mail-order sale to a given customer. The repeat sales bring in the profits. If you can build a good mailing list by ads for mail-order goods the potential is endless. Assuming you have done a good job, and made an honest presentation in your ad, the person who bought from you for the first time is pleased with what he got and is very likely to buy from you again.

So far, plans for advertising include: (1) the necessary funds budgeted to advertise for at least three consecutive issues (you are reconciled to the fact that you will do well if you get enough orders to break even on the cost of the ads); (2) brochures, listings, catalogs, or other literature ready to include with all orders. What should come next?

The question of timing must be considered. Copy usually has to reach the publisher at least six weeks before publication date. Sometimes, this lead time is as much as three months. It is therefore important to plan the time for your ad to be placed so that it will be most effective. Timing for ads depends largely upon the nature of the items offered. Some things are just naturals for Christmas gifts, so exposure should begin in September. If your handcrafts have special applications to vacations, since June, July, and August are the heavy vacation months, your advertisement should come out in April, May, and June. If you consider a minimum of six weeks' lead time for an ad aimed at vacationers, you should place the first some time in

February. Consequently, the earliest possible orders to come from that February advertisement will be in April, and more likely May.

As you examine this problem from all sides, you will naturally want to consider assistance from an advertising agency. The function of the agency is to assist in the preparation and placement of the advertising, for which their fee is generally about 15 percent of the cost of the ad. Most publications allow you to deduct agency fees from your payment for the ad.

Unless you have a much larger budget than most craftsmen who are thinking of placing their first ads, you will find that 15 percent of the cost of your ad will generate little action on the part of any advertising agency. Should you plan on spending several thousand dollars, that becomes another matter. But for those first small ads, agencies cannot justify an effort worth $100 for a fee of $5. One might argue that since the cost of the agency fee is deducted from the ad cost, you really won't have to spend anything for the service of an agency. True, but under the circumstances, you will not receive much help either. You might be able to wheedle superficial advice from the agency. However, your advertisements should be planned with care and consideration. Anything less could mean a poor return for your advertising money.

If there is any question in your mind, call an agency and tell them you are ready to begin your first advertising. Tell the person on the other end of the line that you are thinking of placing a $40 ad in *Family Circle*, and ask him how he can help. Be prepared for a prolonged silence. He does not want to be too blunt about it. How can he tell you the truth, that for a fee of $6 he can hardly give you the time of day? Analyze his lack of response. His silence is saying, "Why don't you handle your own ads now and come back later when you have a budget that interests us?"

In conclusion, you must determine your policy concerning complaints. When you sell via mail order, sooner or later you will have complaints. Perhaps it is totally the fault of the customer, who did not read the advertisement carefully in the first place. How are you going to respond to these complaints?

If we assume that you are proud of your work, an honest craftsperson in the broadest use of the term, you will never want anyone to have something of yours unless they are pleased with it. The question of *why* they are not pleased is not relevant. You can point out that somewhere in the ad you noted that all sales were final. You can make that stick. But you cannot turn off the complaints. Cranks will do anything and everything possible to harass you. They can get the ear of the Better Business Bureau and automatic sympathy from any consumer protection bureau. This is because, to the agency hearing the complaint, you are automatically suspect if you sell by mail order.

There is a reason for this attitude. For instance, a great many of the ads concerning how to make money at home in your spare time are outright swindles of one sort or another. Those who live off such rackets are generally careful to avoid any obvious violation of the law. They are not at all worried about how many complaints come in, so long as the other suckers send in the small monies.

In my opinion, the best way is the simplest way. Offer your handcrafts with an unconditional guarantee: satisfaction or money back. The chances are that you will rarely hear complaints. I have followed this practice for a considerable period of time with a quite varied product line. In fact, there have been so few complaints that each stands out as a vivid memory.

Now we will consider the alternate method of using the mails to sell: direct-mail advertising. In this case, you prepare a brochure, flier, pamphlet, or catalog and mail it to a list of people who might be interested.

The shotgun approach, mailing to any group of citizens, is hardly to be recommended. It makes much more sense to send your listing to those interested. Where do you go for help in such a venture?

Almost every city now has some kind of printing and mailing service. These people are in the business of supporting operations such as yours. They have lists broken down into profession, occupation, income bracket—almost every way you can imagine. For a small charge, something like five cents a name, they will sell you the listing of your choice. If you want total service, they will take your raw copy, turn it into printed literature, then address and mail the fliers for you.

When you evaluate such a service, you might conclude that you can do it yourself at far less cost. Perhaps your direct cost would be less, but there are certain items you just cannot get around, no matter how you try.

The flier, brochure, listing, catalog, or whatever you finally choose, has to be printed and collated. It is almost always folded, then stamped or enclosed in some kind of envelope. The address must be on the cover or envelope.

Even when you do all of this labor yourself, it will be costly. You can estimate that total expenses for any kind of direct-mail campaign (except when mailing third class in extremely large volume—by the millions) will be no less than $1 per name and may well creep as high as $3. Let us assume that you plan to mail 1,000 direct-mail fliers detailing what handcrafts you have available (remember to add packing and shipment charges to your normal retail price). Just how well must you do in order to break even?

We will assume that each piece of literature in the mail (which cost you exactly $1) lists several handcrafted items that retail at an average of $5. If you have priced these items correctly, you, the craftsman, will expect to wholesale them for $2.50 to the direct-mail distributor—that is, you wearing another hat.

Now for an analysis of the cost of the mailing. As the merchandiser, you receive 50 percent of the retail price. Thus, to pay for the direct expense of $1,000, you must sell sufficient items to generate $2,000. An average retail order of $5 could cost 50¢ to process and ship. Thus, to break even on initial costs you must process no less than 400 orders. Your cost of 50¢ on these orders is another $200. Now the break even point is $2,200.

With each average sale producing $5, you require some 440 orders for that $2,200 income; or, one out of every five people who receive your mailing must buy.

Herein lies the crux of mail-order advertising. The national average is 3 percent return from mail-order advertising. In the above calculations, we were anticipating a 20 percent return in order to break even. Let us suppose you have a fine product and do an exceptional job of reaching your potential customers. You double the national average—quite an accomplishment. Where does that leave you? With a great big 6 percent.

Since the mailing we were discussing comprised 1,000 orders, 6 percent would mean 60 checks for $5. This means a total income of $300. Since you are purchasing the items at wholesale, your cost to fill the 60 retail orders is $150. Therefore, mailing and wholesaling costs total $1,150. Your return (at double the national average, remember) is $300.

Obviously, there is simply no way for you to find any profit from that operation. Costs are some four times the anticipated income. The more you mail, the more you lose. The harder you work at this merchandising effort, the more it will cost you.

The maxim is, mail-order sales must be repeated constantly if they are to generate any income. Never regard mail order as a one-time operation. Either embark on a long campaign of mail order or employ a different sales method.

If you do intend to use mail-order advertising to sell your handcrafts, you must have a constantly updated list of merchandise, new items must be added regularly, and frequent mailings of your lists have to be sent to the customers.

The advantages of the printing and mailing service now become even more obvious. New fliers will have to be mailed regularly to your prospective customers—you hardly have the time to handle this work, if you are to design new products and continue to produce the original items.

The actual facts for mail-order advertising are that unless you have the funds to support at least three mailings to your selected lists, you cannot reach a break even point. Therefore, unless you have the capacity to develop new items continually, you will lose your customers after they have seen your first listing.

Perhaps this type of selling is right for you. Once again, a great deal depends on your craft and your personal approach. So long as you can satisfy the above requirements, you will maintain a level of income necessary to support yourself from your handcraft sales. Just be certain that you do indeed qualify for this rather specialized and initially costly selling method.

National average is 3% return on mail order solicitations. solicitations.

11

Some Special Situations: Leagues, Associations, Groups, Juried Shows

The individual who wishes to become self-supporting through selling his wares is always searching for an organized group that can offer him assistance. Perhaps the most prominent is the American Craft Council, a national organization and the group sponsoring *Craft Horizons*. The stated purpose of the ACC is to assist American craftsmen.

Undoubtedly, the ACC is of value, through such services as their annual list of craft shops that buy wholesale and/or accept crafts on consignment. However, they tend to emphasize the unique or singular items. I personally feel that the pieces this council selects are too far out for the average person. Certainly, the ACC favors crafts that are definitely art-oriented rather than the more usual crafts. There is a place for crafts of the hothouse type but fortunately, the common garden variety of crafts will always be in popular demand.

Many local craft organizations take their cue from the American Craft Council. Although such groups are ostensibly organized to assist the beginning craftsmen, they usually show the same exclusive emphasis as ACC. One such organization in the Northwest has the wonderful name, Friends of the Crafts. The membership is composed largely of wealthy socialites. You would naturally expect that their annual craft sale would be a bonanza for the craftsperson. Actually, it's a bust. Mighty little is bought during the afternoon of the big important social event, which is free to participating handcrafters. This group also sponsors special exhibits for their gallery. As one would expect, many of these are quite singular and far removed from what you are likely to be interested in making.

One swiftly learns to sort out the organizations that are more social than anything else. They emphasize known artists in the craft fields, they specialize in social events, and the local publicity releases are excellent—but little is done to aid the beginning hobbyist. No special value is attached to the fact that you are a member of such an organization. Nobody cares except a few at the top of the social ladder. Membership in such a group offers few benefits indeed.

In contrast, a number of regional groups have been extremely successful in helping the craftsman. Perhaps the best known are in the mountains of the Southeast. Hundreds of mountain people have been helped to continue producing craft items indigenous to the area. Also of great importance is the fact that the skills involved are preserved.

The organization that is really going to help the individual start selling his work will be characterized by such activities as assistance in buying supplies, craft classes, and national catalogs. The classes will be highly practical and aimed at offering the hobbyist new information and fresh skills for the craft field of his choice. The cost of such classes will be modest—within the reach of anyone who is really interested.

In addition, expert assistance in buying a selection of necessary tools and equipment for your craft—often at a price somewhat below normal retail—is of immense value. Even more important is quantity buying of craft supplies. This is where that vital cost break comes. To a certain degree, such organizations are like a cooperative, but they are usually sponsored by some governmental agency.

The third major assistance offered the craftsman is help in selling. Regions are catalogued and sales efforts made nationally. The producing handcrafter has an established market. For instance, the efforts to aid the craftsmen of the North American Indians are very well developed. For those of us who do not belong to a particular ethnic group or live in a specific geographic area, there are as yet few craft organizations. Fortunately, people through the country seem to have a great interest in establishing such leagues or groups.

Every craft magazine one picks up has another article on this subject. Undoubtedly, such organizations—when they are eventually created—will be local or regional initially. It is not likely that funds will be available to promote them. However, growth from local and regional to national could come within the next five years or so.

Any organizations that develop in this manner are very likely to do much for the handcrafter. One hopes there will be a strong orientation toward the crafts rather than the fine arts. It is this type of group that will really make it possible for the American Craftsman to come of age.

Now for a few comments on the type of show

where awards are made for craft entries. The juried show as it currently exists is a natural outgrowth of the fine art aspect of the arts-crafts festival. The extension of the use of the jury to craft products is relatively new but seems to be growing. The jury previews all items submitted for the festival, selects the winners for the awards and, in many cases, makes the decision as to which items are acceptable for the show.

Unfortunately, standards by which the jury makes decisions rarely exist; naturally, there is going to be wide variations in the pattern. The relatively small local art festival just getting started will ordinarily have a jury composed of people teaching on the college level in a related subject. Since this struggling festival is short of funds, the probability is that the jury will not be paid and, as there is little status to this type of festival as yet, it is likely to be a jury of one.

Comes the preview and the jury of one makes the decisions. At this point, the inevitable personal prejudices of the one-man jury take their toll. There is no such thing as a person without some bias, but rejection can be a crushing blow to the individual who has submitted his work.

Even if there are a number of jurors, the situation doesn't really change. There will almost always be a dominant person whose prejudices can lead to the same result as that of the one-man jury. One year, an art festival in the Pacific Northwest didn't have a single painting with blue in it. You should not have to be told why. It is pretty obvious, isn't it? The juror whose views dominated the group just did not like blue.

Thus the pattern emerges. Wherever there is a juried show, there are likely to be inconsistencies and decisions based on prejudice. To some degree, of course, there is no way around this. It is certainly unlikely to change until standards, either regional or national, are set. Perhaps the best course for the craftsperson is obvious: participate in a juried show only if you honestly believe rejection would not bother you.

The so-called "screening" of craftsmen's work by local volunteer committees is not very different from the juried show. In sharp contrast is a type of festival which seems relatively rare. A description of the one conducted by the Chamber of Commerce, University District, Seattle, Washington, gives the idea. The festival was not advertised in the name of fine art. While it is arts-crafts, it is dominated by business people. Of course, their system has some limitations and drawbacks, but in other ways it is delightful. A given area of the street is roped off for the festival. The stalls are lined out and numbered on the street. Each is the same size. Those who wish to participate are accepted upon payment of a modest fee per booth. The participant may have one or several locations if he so chooses. Stalls are assigned as applications are received.

From that point on, it is pretty much as you name it. There is no screening committee, no judge, no rules concerning nature of display, decoration of booth, etc. (frequently, there is a requirement that each stall be removed at a stated hour each night). In this festival, there is a great mixture of quality and products. Probably there is little that anyone would recognize as fine art. So the carnival atmosphere is appropriate. If the hobbyist who has paid to participate brings junk that doesn't sell, that is his problem. In the long run, this well-organized yet seemingly casual show may be an answer in part to craft selling. One thing is sure, the attitude of the crowds at this type of show is different. Everyone is doing his own thing. The crowd not only recognizes this but apparently is in complete agreement that this is the way it should be. Thus the heckling and smart remarks associated with festivals are uncommonly rare at this type of event.

12

Custom Orders

The area of custom orders is, in my opinion, one of the most important for craftsmen with regard to income-producing, quality work. Today, a great deal of emphasis, even prestige, is given handcrafted work, especially when it is a custom order. I feel that no handcrafter who wishes to become self-supporting should fail to take advantage of the opportunities for custom orders. However, because of the readily apparent problems, mainly those of communication and rapport, many craftsmen are reluctant to undertake such work.

One of the most surprising things of all is that you will find custom orders coming to you long before you may feel qualified for such work—often almost as soon as you begin showing your craftwork. As with any other type of selling, it is important that you analyze what to expect and how to handle the details of custom work *before* the first such order is undertaken.

When someone commissions a custom order, it is vital that you and the potential customer really communicate. If you fail to understand what the customer thought he told you, the sale is lost; and you may have created a poor impression as well. Verbal communication alone is often inadequate. A sketch of the proposed work is the best answer. If you are capable of doing quick drawings that give a feel for your work, it would be wise to make that standard practice for all custom orders. Be sure to use the actual color, if one is suggested. This is one of the most difficult areas when there is nothing but words to go on. People who want a particular color tone can be most definite about it and often will not accept the slightest deviation.

If possible, some kind of scale model is even better than a drawing. A sample of a woven fabric, an unfired model of the pottery ordered, anything that is really representative of the item(s) ordered. If possible, the model or sample should be relatively finished and the colors used as planned for the completed items.

The jeweler has an easy time of it in this respect. It is not difficult to outline a custom order and ask the client to return in a few days to see a wax model of the proposed jewelry. Of course, if the model has been mended and patched in several different colors of wax that may take a bit of explaining, but if the model is sprayed lightly with gold, it conveys a good idea of the item to be produced.

When it comes to accepting custom orders, there are potential hazards as well as important rewards. You no doubt have developed a certain style, a way of treating the materials of your craft; you can do that well and you enjoy it. Perhaps you also avoid certain techniques practiced in the same craft. For instance, when making a jewelry model, my inclination is toward the organic or free form. I soon learned that it was best not to accept a custom order if it was to be different from my normal style. No matter how capable one is, no matter how well the job is done, if one has no enjoyment from the crafting, the order is not worthwhile. Also, if one does not enjoy handling such a custom order, often there's a better than even chance that the customer also will not be pleased with the finished item.

In the long run, it is best to decline firmly an order that you will not enjoy handling. Just face up to it, "Now that I understand exactly what you want, it's obvious it isn't the type of thing I normally do. I suggest that you talk with someone else." If you can offer the name of a suitable craftsman, by all means do so. Both you and the potential customer will be the better for your having declined this job.

Another extremely important consideration has to do with your financial arrangement. It is the general practice to accept a down payment when the commission is initially proposed. Perhaps 10 to 20 percent of the price of the item. When a known artist accepts an important commission, this advance payment can be quite substantial.

Nothing is wrong with the idea of accepting a portion of the fee in advance—it certainly helps separate the genuine clients from those who are just talking. But despite the fact that such down payment is common practice, the writer prefers not to accept such. And there is a most important reason for this: when no down payment has been accepted, no contractual obligation to the customer exists. Acceptance of money toward a job constitutes a legal contract, verbal though it may be. Of course, few customers are going to get legal about such a contract, but when no payment has been accepted, the degree of obligation to the client is less than if down payment has been taken.

I learned this the hard way and then had it confirmed by the experience of others. When you fail to please a customer with a piece of custom work, the chances are even that you'll never please that customer—no matter how many times you rework the item. Here again, this fact was gained through sad experience. There is no logical explanation for this, but once you fail to please a customer the first time, you are likely to find that nothing you can do in the future will please him.

This is the approach to avoid acceptance of the down payment. "No, I don't want any money now. You see, I will create something that will be pleasing to me. If you find you do not like it, I do not want the obligation of reworking it for you."

Many craftsmen flatly refuse to consider custom orders. While there is a very good reason for this unwillingness, one must also consider the considerable advantages.

One can easily understand why many are negative on the subject. It seems that no matter how carefully the handcrafter tries to communicate with the customer, it is apparent there was a failure when the finished work is seen. "Why, that does not look at all like I expected it to." This comment is to be anticipated. It will happen where custom work is done.

Sometimes this problem arises because the customer was not able to visualize the end result. Often, he is not sure just what he wants, and the communication breakdown can occur regardless of the amount of effort expended: sketches, drawings, and so forth may be adequate generally but not always. One would think that the wax model would be a virtually foolproof device, especially when it is explained to the client that the finished object will be precisely similar to the model in every detail. However, this is not always the case.

It is, of course, these relatively few problems that scare craftsmen away from custom work.

Most of the people who place such orders are pleasant to work with and most appreciative of the end results. Therein lies one of the rewarding aspects of such commissions.

Another facet of custom work should also be noted. The customer comes into the studio shop, finds that custom work is handled, and says, "I was in San Francisco the other day and saw a ring that I really wanted. Now I wish I had bought it—but I'm sure you can make me one like it." For the word ring you can substitute jug, coat, tapestry, stained glass lantern—the list is virtually endless. However, whatever the craft item—and however intrigued you may be with the possibilities of such a custom order—run up the red flag, step on the alarm buzzer, and be alert. This is one of the worst custom situations you can become involved with. This eager customer wants an exact duplicate of an item that you have never seen. She has the advantage, because she has seen it.

Under these circumstances, should you rely on the customer's untrained eye and glowing memory? Can you honestly expect to duplicate something you have never seen and which is being described to you in nontechnical terms by someone totally unaware of the work involved in that particular craft? If you should accept this job be prepared. You do not have one chance in a hundred that it will meet the customer's approval. The best course of action is to beat a hasty retreat. Gently but firmly inform the customer that she has an advantage: she has seen it and you have not. You might comment, "When you see something you like, you should buy it because you might not have another chance at the same item." Obviously, there is plenty of room for differences of opinion regarding this. You may wish to attempt to sell the customer something else. I do not. While I do not exactly try to push the client out of the studio, I absolutely do not have the slightest desire to try to sell her a substitute for the desired item. If the customer browses and finds an acceptable substitute that is another matter entirely.

A few words about pricing custom work. Several factors must be considered. You are expected to create a unique item, one that will not be duplicated. This has a certain value which tends to increase the price. On the other hand, you assume that the customer will like the work and therefore pay promptly. This means there is no inventory problem and no large stock has to be carried for months.

Then there is the question of how long the work will take. If you are familiar with the techniques required—and as we discussed previously, time and motion studies are an essential factor for the handcrafter who aims to become self-supporting—you should be able to estimate the time required, along with the materials, rather accurately. Pricing thus can be based upon all of these considerations.

If the work entails learning new techniques—thus gaining new skills—you can hardly expect the customer to pay for this learning time. Make your best estimate of how long it would take you to do the job if you already had the required skills. Base your price on that and then write off the hours required to learn the techniques as part of your own investment in becoming a more capable craftsman.

Custom work will enrich your skills enormously. You will also be amazed at some of the design ideas that emerge from such orders. So by all means emphasize your ability in this area. Just make certain that you stay in control. You will so long as you are aware of the many ramifications of the situation.

13

Repairing Handcrafted Products

The repair of handcrafted products is an extremely interesting field in many ways. People everywhere have some item no longer functioning that they would like repaired. Most of the major craft activities thus offer possibilities for a repair service. Since few places are willing to undertake the repair of leather goods, weavings, jewelry, ceramics, etc., the craftsman who will may generate quite a business.

When you consider setting up your own repair service and investigate the advantages and disadvantages, you will end up with mixed emotions. As with custom work, certain trouble areas exist and have to be negotiated with extreme care.

We will cover the positive factors first: (1) there is always a considerable amount of work to be done; (2) repairs increase your skills tremendously; (3) goodwill can be generated. Since your aim is to become self-supporting, item (1) will certainly help your income. Item (2) means that as you constantly face the challenge of how to accomplish the repair, you evolve new techniques and become more proficient. I'm afraid that is the sum total of the good points of repair work.

My following comments are pretty negative. For one thing, the object to be repaired is frequently of little tangible value. While this is not necessarily true always, it seems that many people who want things repaired are in somewhat strained economic circumstances. These facts add up to the probability that the person wants the repair at very low cost. Of course, there are important exceptions. The restoration of art objects, and such is usually a most lucrative field, especially if commercial enterprises or collectors are involved. In such cases, money is no object.

However, the average repair service is unlikely to bring in enough to meet your self-imposed hourly rate. Also, you have no way of knowing whether the item will withstand your repair treatment—perhaps it will collapse totally. You must be willing to face the customer afterwards and say, "I really tried my best but I regret to tell you I've wrecked your treasured antique." At that point, no matter how sorry you are, no matter how nice the customer is, you will hardly have good references from that client. It adds up to this, in my opinion: you stand to lose more than you gain.

Should you still be willing to forge ahead, keep the following considerations in mind. The mechanics of the order should be handled methodically. A repair ticket is essential. This indicates the item, customer's name, what is to be done, the due date, and so on. One of the vital details is the value of the item. You can probably get by without this and never end up with a serious problem. If you should do so, recognize that you are taking a risk.

The possibility exists that when something goes wrong, the irate customer will take legal action.

Perhaps the most important detail on that repair ticket has to do with whether or not the item has sentimental value. If you do not put down any other detail, always obtain this fact. You can probably forget the customer's name, and what you were supposed to do—and yet be able to talk your way out of it. But wreck a valueless item of sentimental worth and you will have an unforgettable lesson. My policy is that if the item has sentimental value, I will not handle it. Sentiment cannot be appraised; similarly, the item cannot be duplicated or replaced.

All illustration is in order. A very pleasant woman brought in a ring for repair. The tangible value lay between 25¢ to 50¢. The lightweight, 10 karat gold band was broken and a tiny pearl was missing from the setting. A simple repair job. It just did not cross my mind that this trinket could have any value, sentimental or otherwise. We scheduled several weeks for the repair. In the usual confusion of the craftsman's studio, the ring was put aside and did not get repaired on the due date. But then, the customer did not come in either. Naturally, that took the pressure off. The job no longer had any priority. Several months later, in came my customer. By then, no one even remembered what the ring looked like; we did not even have the slightest idea of its whereabouts. We were all most cordial. Miss —— was told, "I am sorry, but we have misplaced your ring and cannot put our hands on it right now. Let us have a look around. Perhaps you can drop back in a day or two?"

After considerable time had been spent in searching for the ring, it became obvious that we had better plan how to appease the customer. The natural thing of course, was to offer a replacement.

So on Miss ———'s return, the explanation was made, regret expressed, and an offer made.

You have probably guessed it already. That is when the explosion came. We were informed in no uncertain terms that the ring was literally priceless. It had very deep sentimental value and we had better stop all other activities until we found the ring. (Such a situation cannot be salvaged. Attempts at appeasement are not only futile, they seem to enrage the customer further.) Finally, I commented as I felt appropriate. "Since it is obvious that you attach what I consider an unreasonable value to this item we have unfortunately lost, I can only suggest that you consult your attorney while I do the same."

Of course, when this happens, one is placed in an impossible situation. Somehow, in this particular case, luck was with us and we found the damn thing. So it ended. But you can be sure of one thing—it won't happen to me again.

It is possible to capitalize upon the growing market for repairs. This suggestion was made by a professional jeweler who had many years of experience. He said that he would not touch a repair himself. However, if he had someone working with him as an apprentice, it could be an effective way of accomplishing several jobs simultaneously: instructing the apprentice and allowing such work to help pay for the person's wage. If a capable employee is part of the organization, this does appear an excellent way to handle repair work.

14

Students: Your Best Advertisement

When you have considered—and perhaps tried —every possible method of merchandising, you probably still haven't exhausted the possibilities. The side effects of teaching will do more for you than any kind of advertising you ever used. In the meantime it can be, and should be, profitable in itself! How's that for a real winner?

The average person is likely to protest that he just is not prepared to teach, has never taught anyone, and furthermore does not know how to go about starting. However, the average craftsman is more creative than other "average" people. He has demonstrated an ability to create with his hands. He has shown the self-confidence and initiative necessary to launch a career in the craft field of his choice. Of course he can teach!

It would be much simpler if someone could help

you in this venture. Unfortunately, there is a scarcity of literature in this field. Once again, I will draw from my experience—all illustrations in this book are real, not dreamed up. Since the field of metalcraft and jewelry is my basic business, I'll illustrate from that craft with regard to teaching.

Of course, it helps that I received an engineering degree a good many years ago. While it was never put to direct use, some of the knowledge is still there. My own experience in taking lessons for metalcraft was poor. My locale had one teacher so the options were limited. The universities had several teachers but such classes were not available to the public.

My instructor does beautiful work. His techniques are excellent and he is also a perfectionist. Everyone was expected to become like him. Thus the first several weeks were spent perfecting several techniques. The final result was a small sterling medallion that was rather blah.

These methods did not change. There was always the demand for perfection coupled with extremely slow progress. Since my temperament is quite different, the relationship did not last too long.

Some years later, my wife and I began to think of teaching. In light of our own experience, we set out with the announced objective that each student would complete an item of jewelry every lesson, beginning with the first. We also organized the course so that it would come to a stopping place at the tenth lesson. We had no desire for professional students.

It really isn't terribly difficult to organize classes so that each student completes a project each lesson. Such progress makes for very high motivation, of course, as well as pleased students—who want everybody to know what they are doing.

In order to have the student complete a project

each lesson, several things must be considered well before the first class.

1. You, as a teacher, must not expect perfection on the first effort. If you are a perfectionist yourself, that's your business. But nothing is more frustrating to a student than a teacher who expects a beginner to accomplish perfect work. So make it very clear to the prospective students that you are teaching *techniques*. And perfection in these techniques will often come only after many, many hours have been spent developing the proper skill of hand and eye.

That does not mean that you want the students' work to be sloppy. It just means that you expect perfection to come later, in the student's own time.

2. Each lesson should be organized around a relatively simple project that does not introduce too many new techniques in one session. Try also to plan the lesson series so that techniques acquired in earlier lessons will contribute to those later in the series. Each technique is just one more "building block" in the student's possession.

In order to keep lessons relatively simple, you must decide what the student will do in each class. The student can have no choice of projects. He cannot begin in the middle of the course but must start at lesson one and work through in proper sequence.

There may be objections that this is arbitrary, that the student should choose his own project. Well, one thing is certain. If the student chooses his own projects, he will almost always pick something far beyond his skill level that requires not just a few but many complex techniques.

Within the framework of the lesson, the student will be given complete freedom. But his project, and the techniques learned, are decided for him.

3. The time limits of each session should be clearly defined. Unless this is established, some students will stay all day and night. Lessons call

for intense concentration on the part of the student. Somewhere between two to three hours seems best. Any less time makes it difficult to complete a project, while a longer session will certainly produce some weary students.

The three points listed above define an approach to teaching. Stay within this framework and you won't go far wrong.

In order to maintain the necessary control over your teaching methods and class sessions, I find that an interview with prospective students before accepting them into classes is preferable. One needs to clarify for those interested in enrolling in your classes that certain procedures have been established and have to be followed.

I have found that certain signs emerge when you are interviewing the student. They are usually very clear, especially if you ask the right questions. I would warn prospective teachers to stay clear of any student who has a sharply defined and limited objective. I once interviewed two young people who wanted to enroll in my jewelry course. It soon became clear that they wanted to make their own wedding rings. Their ideas on this subject were quite decided.

I felt that I could not accept them as students. Why? Because never in this world would they have been pleased with their efforts. They had a clear mental image of what they wanted, but their hands and eyes had no skills. You might say that they were high-school students who wanted to begin with postgraduate courses.

Also be very slow to enroll a student who is a perfectionist. He'll assure you that he will accept your method and that he *will* get his project completed, even though he recognizes ahead of time that it will not be perfect. What he did not tell you is that he will be unhappy with every item that he produces. Obviously unhappy! Such a person can

teaching license/ may be required.
permit

cause a group of beginner students to go sour more rapidly than anything I know.

The preceding are the basic ground rules for planning your lessons. The final consideration is the size of the class. If you have assistance, you can more than double the number you can teach alone. If I am by myself, I feel that three students is a maximum in metalcraft courses. If I have capable assistance, that number can go up to a total of ten (five students for each skilled teacher).

Most classes enroll far higher numbers than those I recommend. They also have many graduates who have learned little. The smaller classes will give both you and the students greater satisfaction.

Now we come to the question of fee. Well, the cost must not be too high or there will be very few students. On the other hand, the costs should not be too low. The prime considerations are your time and the equipment involved. Beginners in a lapidary class can wreck a good grinding wheel in five minutes. They can go through quite a few such wheels in the course of a few weeks. This must be anticipated and priced into the lessons. The materials used must also be part of the price structure.

It has been my practice to include materials in all jewelry classes. This may not work in some craft fields but it certainly makes life a lot simpler for me. Here again, it is more of that control necessary to meet the objectives of the teaching method.

Some cities and states require that you apply for a teaching permit. Most such permits are required when the teaching is a form of vocational training, in which case such requirements do not apply to you. Obviously, you should check the laws in your region.

In the field of jewelry and metalcraft, our own printed lessons have been used by several hundred correspondence students. A number of these former students have used the same literature to establish their own classes. Complex skills *can* be communicated in written form, and there are indications that the correspondence students do better than students attending lessons. Since the former have nothing but the written word, they are forced to return to it instead of casually asking—and casually listening—in class.

Most students are very appreciative of your efforts. If you are thorough in interviewing and screening before accepting students, you will probably have only fruitful teaching experiences.

15

Searching for Supplies

A list of suppliers in the many fields of arts and crafts would be of little value without some indication of how these suppliers operate. A few are organized for quick and effective direct-mail service even on small orders. Others have totally different methods. In some cases, the listings are free; in many, there is a charge which applies to the listing but can be credited to the first order for materials.

Since this book deals with the very broad field of all crafts, rather than concentrating on a specific endeavor, the effort to offer an exhaustive listing of sources would unfortunately be impossible.

It has long been difficult for the craftsman to obtain much assistance in this area. But with the rapidly increasing number of craftsmen, there will undoubtedly be compilations of sources in some depth.

Regardless of how you obtain source information, two steps will help you in its use:

1. A printed letterhead for your business is important. It is not essential to be incorporated —you can still use the name, ABC Craft Company. While the terminology is generally accepted without question, it has little legal significance in many states. You are still fully responsible for anything that pertains to your company and its products.

2. Always maintain a separate bank account for your business. Print your retail sales tax license number on the checks (see Chapter 3). There is no better way to be accepted by organizations that normally do not sell to individual craftsmen.

Now you are ready to deal with your sources. You should understand that there are several major categories of possible sources, and that each may require a different approach.

MAIL-ORDER SUPPLIERS

Several distinctly different types of mail-order suppliers exist. The question of which one is right for you depends upon the nature of your products and the amount of business you are handling.

Major National Suppliers

Such suppliers generally have a network of distributors and rarely sell to individuals. This is because their facilities are not geared to handling small individual orders. However, if you inquire *on your letterhead*, stating clearly what you produce, the chances are that even the largest suppliers will be glad to accept you on a minimum order basis.

As I have mentioned previously (see Chapter 3), it is not good policy to buy everything from one source. Therefore, it is usually preferable to buy from the major supplier only those items required in some quantity. The majority of such suppliers will, after your first order, bill your company on a monthly basis.

Area or Regional Suppliers

These localized suppliers usually serve a network of retail outlets, on a level below the national supplier. While such mail-order houses may carry on business in every part of the country, generally it is centered in one region. Of course, the increasing cost of shipment of goods is a major reason for the setup of this type of distributor. Where considerable weight is involved, shipping costs become a significant factor.

The area or regional supplier occasionally sells to individuals by direct mail. Generally it is wise to make inquiries on your letterhead. If any discount is available from this level of distributors, it varies widely.

General Suppliers

This group of suppliers is in the business of direct mail to individuals. There is no mistaking them —they are very aggressive in merchandising and generally offer excellent service. Since they operate on the basis of payment accompanying the order, all discount information is given in the catalog.

Do not overlook this third type of mail-order house. Compare their prices for similar merchandise in both the area and national listings. This type of supplier is seldom concerned about brand-name merchandise. They may be able to supply equivalent items at about the same price as the large suppliers.

This fourth type of mail-order house handles only sharply limited sections of the craft fields. However, they often cover their market in greater depth than the previous type of suppliers. This is of course invaluable to the producing craftsman.

When you need assistance in use of products, turn to these specialists. They are generally pleased to offer advice. Obviously, the supplier who handles several overlapping craft fields can hardly be expert on everything he lists—such distributors depend almost completely upon information furnished by *their* sources. The specialized supplier, on the other hand, usually can be of great assistance concerning the use of his products.

Sources other than mail order are necessarily local. In this context, local includes the nearest metropolitan center—the one most likely to be visited frequently. Usually, quite varied local sources are available, many of them almost unknown to the average handcrafter.

GENERAL CRAFT RETAILERS

These shops fall into several distinct categories. Most carry a broad range of supplies for the hobbyist craftsman. Your local telephone directory will carry them under the following listings:

> Arts and Crafts Suppliers
> Art Supplies
> Hobby and Model Construction Supplies

The fact that the telephone book has no listing for "craft stores" does not mean that there are none. However, these shops carry a very broad range of items and thus are often thought of as suppliers either to the artist or the hobbyist.

Do not neglect the art suppliers. They will have many items that may interest you. Art is no longer separated into rigid categories; today the "painter" who uses material, found objects, or perhaps acrylic thread on his canvas has every chance of being exhibited and purchased by national art galleries—quite a change from the days of the strict academy rules. One often finds that the art supplier has a broader line of useful merchandise than some of the craft or hobby shops.

Perhaps the broadest, most general category of all is the chain store. One such network is the familiar American Handicraft, whose shops seem to cater to people who fall somewhere between the hobbyist and the artist—in other words, they can satisfy just about everyone's needs.

SPECIALTY CRAFT RETAILERS

Numerous specialized suppliers also serve the crafts. Here are the listings under which they will be found in telephone and reference directories:

> Art Needlework Materials
> Beads
> Ceramics
> Lapidary Equipment and Supplies
> Rocks, for Collectors

This category still serves the hobbyist, craftsman, and artist. Few of these shops supply industry or trade. Like all shops of this nature, they are likely to have items that will be of interest to the producing craftsman. Today, the number of manufacturers of equipment and supplies in this field is growing so rapidly that no one can really keep abreast of the many developments. A quick and perhaps regular survey of such outlets should be of constant benefit.

INDUSTRIAL SUPPLIERS

Perhaps the most important category of all is that of the suppliers of industrial equipment and supplies. This category is generally not familiar to the handcrafter. It is at this point that your letterhead and/or checks with your company name and tax license number really produce results. Many such suppliers have the policy of selling wholesale only. However, they are also usually most cooperative if approached in a positive and businesslike manner. After all, policy can be interpreted in a broad manner—so long as it does not require another set of accounting ledgers. There are numerous listings to be investigated.

Abrasives
Acids
Adhesives
Alloys
Aluminum Products
Art Metal
Asbestos Products
Boxes
Brass
Brick, Fire
Bronzes
Buffing and Polishing
    Supplies
Chemicals
Clay, and Clay Products
Dental Equipment and
    Supplies
Diamonds, Industrial
Dye and Dyestuffs
Electrical-Electronic
    Supplies
Engravers
Fiber and Fiber Products
Foil and Foil Products
Foundries and Foundry
    Products

Gas, Liquefied Petroleum
Glass, Fiber
Glass, Stained and Leaded
Glass, Plate and Window
Gloves, Work and
    Industrial
Glues
Grinding Machinery and
    Equipment
Grinding Wheels
Hardware
Hardwoods
Insulation Materials
Jewelry
Junk Dealers
Lubricants
Mailing Containers
Metal Finishing
    Equipment and
    Supplies
Metals, Precious
Paper
Plastics
Plating Equipment and
    Supplies
Refractories

Rubber Products
School Supplies
Scrap Metal
Silks
Smelting and Refining,
    Precious Metals
Screen Printing
    Equipment and
    Supplies

Surplus Merchandise
Textiles
Tools
Tubing
Wax
Wire
Yarn

A few illustrations concerning the use of this list are in order. Suppose you need a relatively small, high-temperature oven or kiln but wish to design your own. Ceramics may well be the best starting point, and you may find possible sources for materials under this listing. However, other industrial suppliers might be consulted. Two very likely headings are: Foundries and Foundry Products; Refractories. In both cases, these industrial suppliers are likely to have materials directly related to the field of ceramics. Often they will have such a wide range of products that you have more choices. The refractories supplier will have—or can get—some form of castable insulating material that isn't likely to be found in the ceramics shop. With castable insulation, a furnace can be poured very easily. The listing for foundry products covers a wide range of items that might be needed when building a high-temperature furnace.

Two other headings could possibly have application in building your own furnace: Brick, Fire, Clay and Clay Products. These just about exhaust the logical possibilities. But now instead of being limited to one listing, Ceramics, you have five possibilities.

The jewelry craftsperson has an especially large group of listings to consider. Whether fabricating with a torch or doing some type of casting, the jeweler is working with various metals and gem materials. Since this list is somewhat lengthy, only brief comments will be made concerning the relationship of the listing to the jewelry craft.

Abrasives—for finishing
Acids—for pickling
   (chemical cleaning)
Adhesives
Alloys
Brass
Bronze
Buffing and Polishing
   Supplies
Chemicals
Dental Equipment and
   Supplies
Jewelry classifications
  Jewelry Castings

Jewelry Casting
   Equipment
Jewelry Mountings
Jeweler's Supplies and
   Findings
Metal Finishing
   Equipment and
   Supplies
Metals, Precious
Plating Equipment and
   Supplies
Smelting and Refining,
   Precious Metals

The majority of the businesses who come under these headings are suppliers who serve both the manufacturing jewelers and the retail jewelry shops. They are accustomed to working with relatively small commercial establishments. Thus, if you are armed with letterhead and/or checks with your retail tax license number, you will not run into any problems buying from such establishments. However, one detail is vital—keep in mind that you must make the initial contact in a positive manner.

Should you approach a supplier in a hesitant way, wondering in your own mind whether or not it is correct for such a source to deal with you, it is almost certain that you will be questioned. Instead, go armed with the confidence that what you are doing is perfectly legitimate and that you are only establishing the fact that you expect every possible assistance. It does make a difference.

It is almost certain that you will at one time or another want an item not available in the places that carry a broad line of craft supplies. When you have no starting point of reference, a problem like this can seem insoluble. However, a telephone call to the industrial listings that might possibly have the type of item desired will often do the job.

SURPLUS YARDS

No more important source exists for the working craftsman. The businesses in this area of surplus and scrap not only have a very wide assortment of items available, they have a quite high turnover. They are frequently staffed by people who are quite knowledgeable in a wide variety of fields. Generally they make a real effort to find something to serve your purpose.

The fact that you will almost certainly save money by buying everything possible from surplus yards is only one of the benefits. The variety of merchandise that ends up in the surplus yard is amazing. If you know your materials and how to make some compromises in design, depending upon available items, you will often be able to get what's needed at a fraction of what your cost would be in a "proper retail outlet."

The more unusual the item you seek, the more likely it is that it will be a great bargain if you find it in surplus. These shops are very much aware of the value of the items in common demand. Thus such surplus items as fractional horsepower electric motors aren't likely to be any great buy even when surplus. But if you need something for which there is no real market, it's another story.

Now which category of craftsman might like to have the "viewer" used in watching the interior of a reactor? The item involved is a very heavy, thick section of high-leaded glass enclosed in a metal frame. The glass is "water clear." The thickness of the viewer is perhaps six inches, with some six inches horizontal view and two inches vertical view. Should you wish to purchase such an item from a supplier in this field, the cost would be staggering. You simply couldn't afford it. But the surplus shop in my neighborhood had it—several, in fact—at the unbelievable price of $2.50 each!

Even if you didn't go looking for such an item, it would be easy to see how it might be put to very good use somehow.

Make a round of these surplus shops and yards on a monthly basis. When you see something that you really need—buy it on the spot. There's no assurance that it will be there a week later when you come back armed with checkbook. Take a check with you on the very first and each subsequent visit. And when you see something you need, buy it.

Make small talk, "visit" with the people in the surplus establishments. Tell them something about what you are doing. They will be highly receptive to the idea that someone is buying their "junk" and putting it to special use. And they can be very helpful. Once they know the type of items you are looking for, they may even call you when a shipment arrives. It never hurts to take time for a pleasant chat with the people who are in the business of buying and selling the kind of things you may need.

Your sources for tools, equipment, and supplies are somewhat limited. So it pays to familiarize yourself with each category of possible source. The savings in dollars is important. Even more important is the ability to find what you need when you need it.

One of the very best ways to keep up with new sources is to read as many craft publications as possible. There are so many new ones springing up that it's impossible to keep up with them, but each has some useful information. The advertisers in such media are geared to serving the hobbyist rather than the industrial user. Take advantage of the wealth of information in such periodicals, and before long you will have a vast amount of source information!

William E. Garrison

Born in Covington, Georgia, William E. Garrison earned his B.S. in mechanical engineering at the Georgia School of Technology and his B.D. in theology at Columbia Seminary. He then served two pastorates in the Southern Presbyterian Church. Next, he turned to engineering administrative work at Boeing where he spent 13 years.

Having always been a dedicated hobbyist, he decided to devote his time completely to his latest hobby—the creation of handcrafted custom jewelry and teaching jewelry metalcrafting.

In addition to his mastery of craft techniques (in such fields as woodworking, plastics, and leather), Bill also began developing new techniques, chemicals, materials, and equipment for the jeweler-hobbyist. He now holds one patent, has several pending, and is making and marketing more than 100 special products for the jeweler and metalworker.

Teaching and writing about his crafts also came easy for Bill. In each of his classes, Bill would announce his objective: each student would *complete* a jewelry project at every lesson, starting with the first. This objective was attained most of the time; and while working with his students, Bill began to understand how to help them sell their work. It soon became commonplace for his beginner students to sell their very first finished item at a price that made both the student and the teacher proud.

Index